ArtScroll Series®

Rabbi Nosson Scherman / Rabbi Meir Zlotowitz

General Editors

Noble Lives

Published by

Mesorah Publications, ltd

Noble Deeds

Captivating stories
and biographical profiles
of spiritual giants

by Dovid Silber

FIRST EDITION
First Impression … February 2002

Published and Distributed by
MESORAH PUBLICATIONS, LTD.
4401 Second Avenue / Brooklyn, N.Y 11232

Distributed in Europe by
LEHMANNS
Unit E, Viking Industrial Park
Rolling Mill Road
Jarow, Tyne & Wear, NE32 3DP
England

Distributed in Australia and New Zealand by
GOLDS WORLD OF JUDAICA
3-13 William Street
Balaclava, Melbourne 3183
Victoria, Australia

Distributed in Israel by
SIFRIATI / A. GITLER — BOOKS
6 Hayarkon Street
Bnei Brak 51127

Distributed in South Africa by
KOLLEL BOOKSHOP
Shop 8A Norwood Hypermarket
Norwood 2196, Johannesburg, South Africa

ISBN:
1-57819-585-3 (hard cover)
1-57819-586-1 (paperback)

Typography by CompuScribe at ArtScroll Studios, Ltd.
Printed in the United States of America by Noble Book Press Corp.
Bound by Sefercraft, Quality Bookbinders, Ltd., Brooklyn N.Y. 11232

Noble Lives
Noble Deeds

is dedicated to the eternal

memory of the

SIX MILLION

קְדוֹשִׁים וּטְהוֹרִים

Who perished during the

dreadful years of rage

5699 / 1939 — 5705 / 1945

הַשֵׁם יִנְקוֹם דָּמָם

May Hashem avenge their blood

RABBI ISRAEL A. PORTUGAL
1315 54TH STREET
BROOKLYN, N.Y. 11219

ישראל אברהם פארטיגול
בהרה"צ ר' אליעזר זוסיא זצוקלל"ה
מסקולעני – כעת בברוקלין יצ"ו

בעזהשי"ת

יום ה' לסדר להעלות נר תמיד י"א אדר א' תש"ס, ברוקלין יצ"ו

שלו' וישע רב לכבוד אהובי וידידי הרבני התורני המופלא בתורה ויראת שמים, בקי וידען ומושך בעט סופרים וכו' מו"ה ר' דוד זילבער נ"י ויזרח ע"ע, חיים ברכה ושלו'.

בנועם קיבלתי הידיעה אשר בעזהשי"ת עומד להדפיס ספרו אשר בשמו יכונה "במעלות קדושים וטהורים", עובדות וסיפורים מגאוני וקדושי תקופתנו שלאחר חורבן אירופה אשר בארץ החיים המה, וגם לרבות מדור מיוחד בתיאור תולדות חייהם בקצירת האומר, בשם "אנשי קודש."

והנה ידוע שתקופתנו היא מהתקופות הכי קשות בתולדות עמנו באבדן מיליוני קדושים וטהורים על קידוש שמו יתברך. ואחר שנות הזעם והסבל כשכל העמים חשבו שהגיע ח"ו קיצו של של עם ה' ועל חיי טוהר של תורת אמת וקיום מצוותי', הקימו גדולים וקדושים אלו מוסדות התורה והיראה והחסד והחינוך כמשנות דור דור כאשר תחזינה עינינו דורות ישרים מבורכים.

ובודאי שדבר גדול עשה מע"כ נ"י לעורר את זכותם, ובפרט כאשר יסדו לפי תקופות השנה ולפי סדר פרשיות התורה, שמדי דברו בם בסעודות שבת ויום טוב יתעוררו שומעיהם לאהבת ה' וליראתו ולכל מדה נכונה. ואברכהו שהקב"ה יעזרו שיזכה להרבות פעלים לתורה ולזכות את הרבים כפי הרגלו מעודו, וכפי שכבר עשה דבר גדול בעמיו בהרבצת התורה בסדרות "זכרנו לחיים טעיפס" על חורש"י. כן יחזקהו השי"ת להמשיך ביתר שאת ויתר עוז, בכח ובריאות השלימות מתוך תענוג ונחת מכל יוצ"ח, בנים ובני בנים עוסקים בתורה ובמצות, ויזכה בתוך"י לחזות בקרוב בישועת ה' ובשמחתו בביאת משיח צדקנו בב"א. בברכת התורה הנצחית, ידידו עוז

הרב אלי' דוב וואכטפויגעל
RABBI ELI DOV WACHTFOGEL
4 Yeshiva Lane
Fallsburg, N.Y. 12733
914 434-2093

בס"ד מוצש"ק לסדר להעלות נר תמיד, תש"ס.

חזיתי ליקירי, ידידי מנוער, כי מדי דברי בו זכור אזכור את התקופה
היפה והנעימה אהבה בתענוגים עת שתינו מבארו באר מים חיים של
גאון דורנו, רשכבה"ג מרן רבי אהרן קוטלר זצוק"ל בישיבה הקדושה
לייקוואוד, ה"ה הרבני הנכבד, אוצר כל מדה נכונה, סופר מהיר ומחנך
נפלא, הרה"ח ר' דוד זילבער שליט"א שעומד להוציא ספר בשם
"במעלות קדושים וטהורים", עובדות וסיפורים מגדולי הדור שעבר
ונספח אליו תולדותיהם בקיצור, בשם "אנשי קודש".

והנה ידוע גודל ההשפעה של סיפורי צדיקים בבחינת גדול שימושה
יותר מלימודה, ובית צדיקים יעמוד לעד, שמה שיוצא מכח אל הפועל
ע"י מעשה מצדיק, קיים לעד ללמוד ולהשפיע לנצח.

וכבר איתמכי גברא למחנך גדול בחסד עליון ע"י סדרת טעיפס על
חמשה חומשי תורה בשם "זכרונו לחיים טעיפס" שנתקבלו באהדה. ועתה
רחש לבו דבר טוב להוציא לאור את ספר הנ"ל שמביא לידי אמונה
טהורה ואהבת התורה ודרישה לשלמות המדות, והוא חיזוק גדול לדורנו
שצריך התחזקות גדולה בענינים נשגבים אלו.

ואמינא יישר פעלו וחפץ ה' בידו יצליח להגדיל תורה ולהאדירה
כהנה וכהנה.

ידידו מוקירו כערכו הרם,

Table of Contents

Preface

"אודה ה׳ בכל לבב" — "I thank *Hashem* with my whole heart" [*Tehillim* 101:1], with the blessing: "שהחיינו וקימנו והגיענו לזמן הזה" — "Who has granted us life, sustained us and enabled us to reach this occasion." I was barely 4 years old when I was deported, together with my parents, to the central terminal from where the trains left to Auschwitz. We arrived at the terminal an hour after the last train had departed. In a sense, our rescue at the time corresponds to the Sages' statement "One can merit his world [existence] in just one hour." In our case, that hour saved our lives, literally.

After many tribulations, when "slaves ruled over us with no redemption from their hand," we were finally liberated with *Hashem's* great mercy. My parents and their four children were the only surviving family from our city, a major Jewish metropolis.

Notwithstanding my tender age, these events left a deep impression on me. I have always contemplated ways to perpetuate, if even in a minor way, the solemn memory of those *kedoshim utehorim* who ascended to heaven in a hail of blood and tears. They have sanctified the name of *Hashem* with unparalleled pain and suffering, and with the absolute conviction that "You are One and Your Name is One and who is like Your people, Israel" a holy nation of martyrs.

"We have become an object of scorn and derision among the nations, we are regarded as sheep led to slaughter, to be killed, destroyed, beaten and humiliated, and despite all this, we have not forgotten Your Name" [from the weekday *Tachanun*]. Even on the verge of death, when they raked our flesh with iron rods at Auschwitz, Treblinka, Babi Yar and their likes, we have consecrated Your Holy Name to the highest degree man can reach: "even if He takes your soul."

One of *Hashem's* great kindnesses is the fact that immediately after the Holocaust, Torah Jewry was able to reorganize and rebuild on a massive, unparalleled scale. Despite the deep, fresh wound, a new generation emerged in *Eretz Yisrael*, in America, in Western Europe and in many communities throughout the world; a generation of *bnai Torah* and Chasiddim dedicating their lives to serve *Hashem*, delving into the intricacies of Torah and the minutest of its details. It is a manifestation of *Hashem's* compassion for His people that even in exile, He has maintained Torah sages of great stature. Despite their own losses, advanced age and frail health, they injected a new spirit of life into emaciated souls, and relinquished their own needs in order to rebuild their nation. *Baruch Hashem,* they have been highly successful in creating a virtuous and righteous generation of which we can all be proud.

It is my firm conviction that one of the strongest bonds between generations is achieved by relating anecdotes of these great sages, especially those who guided us on the path leading to *Hashem's* service after the horrible *churban*. These stories are a rich source of *yiras Shomayim* and inspiration to lofty traits; teaching us how to climb the ladder of self-perfection to reach intelligence, strength, richness and honor, as defined by the Sages in *Pirkei Avos*: "Who is wise? He who learns from every person. Who is strong? He who subdues his personal desires. Who is rich? He who is happy with his lot. Who is honored? He who honors others."

Sages throughout history have extolled the virtues of relating stories of *tzaddikim*. The *Tiferes Shlomo* states, "discussing their greatness [that of the sages] is the will of *Hashem* and is tantamount to learning Torah" (*Parshas Chayei Sarah*). The renowned Brisker Rav, Harav Chaim Soloveitchik, often said that relating stories about *gedolei Yisrael* is equivalent to the study of *mussar*. His son, Harav Yitzchok Zev Soloveitchik, testified that the single greatest factor responsible for the high level of *yiras Shomayim* among his students was their custom of relating stories of the great sages they knew, such as the Chofetz Chaim, Rav Chaim Ozer Grodzinski of Vilna, Rav Shimon Shkop, *Rosh Yeshivah* of Grodno, and other Torah sages of that remarkable era.

On a personal level, I recall with great fondness sharing the Yom Tov table with my illustrious *Rosh Yeshivah*, Harav Aaron Kotler, *zt"l*. Indeed, what a beautiful sight it was to witness the *Rosh Yeshivah's* radiance and inner joy as he related anecdote after anecdote of Jewry's greatest leaders. In those sublime moments, we so vividly visualized being in Pressburg in the company of the Chasam Sofer; from there, we hopped over to Warsaw to the inner circle of the Chidushei HoRim. Having stopped briefly at the court of Harav Yehoshua Leib Diskin, Chief Rabbi of Yeushalayim, we found ourselves in the company of the Gaon of Vilna, accompanied by his outstanding disciples, Rav Chaim and Rav Zalmale of Volozhin. Those precious moments gave all of us great inspiration and a sincere desire to reach the peak of our spiritual potentials.

This book is my attempt to share this experience. The reader will please note that throughout the book there are quotations of dialogues. Needless to say, they do not record the conversations verbatim; rather they attempt to convey the sense of those conversations.

I take this opportunity to express my sincerest gratitude to *Hashem* for enabling me to publish this first volume of anecdotes in English (translated from the Hebrew volume) about our great *tzaddikim* (the first Hebrew version was titled *B'Maalos Kedoshim Utehorim*); as well as for the great *z'chus* I have had in creating the *Zochreinu LeChaim* tape series on the entire *Chumash/Rashi* in Yiddish.

I wish to thank *Hashem* for having led me on the right path to merit a closeness to my distinguished *rebbe*, *HaGaon*

HaTzaddik Rav Aaron Kotler *zt"l*, *Rosh Yeshivah* of Kletzk and of Beth Medrash Govoha in Lakewood. I was fortunate to drink from his wellspring of Torah in Lakewood. I was also fortunate to benefit from the infinite warmth and affection of my distinguished Rebbe, *HaGaon HaTzaddik* Rav Eliezer Zusia Portugal, the Skulener Rebbe *zt"l*, and that of his son, the present Skulener Rebbe, *shlita*.

Their fiery enthusiasm for every nuance of Torah, their selfless dedication to every altruistic endeavor and their total, unconditional love for Hashem's Chosen People have been etched on my soul forever. May they be our emissaries in heaven to expedite our deliverance through the coming of *Moshiach Tzidkeinu* in the immediate future.

I also wish to express my gratitude to my life's partner, Faigy (Faige Sarah), née Fried, who has stood at my side throughout the years and has encouraged me in every creative endeavor including the present work. May *Hashem* grant us *hatzlachah* in all our endeavors and true *nachas* from all of our offspring.

He Who blessed our forefathers — may He bless the children:

— Our son Chaim Yekusiel Yehuda (Zalman Leib) and his wife Sarah, daughter of Reb Gershon Avraham Klein, and their children, Chizkiya Menachem Manish, Moshe, Eliezer Zusia, Esther Eidl and Yosef Ezra.

— Our son Aaron Moshe and his wife Charna Reizl, daughter of Reb Chaim Mandelbaum, and their precious children, Malky, Rivka Roise and Yisroel.

— Our son Avrohom and his wife Rivka Shaindl, daughter of Reb Shmaya Rieger, and their precious children, Ruchel, Yosef and Yehoshua Zev.

— Our son Mordechai Zvi and his wife Chava, daughter of Reb Pinchas Dovid Rosenberg, and their precious children, Chana and Malka Beila.

— Our son Yechiel and his wife Rivka, daughter of Reb Yaakov Eliezer Kohn.

— Our son Levi Yitzchak.

May I conclude with *Yaakov Avinu's* prayer: "*Hashem* Who shepherds me from my inception until this day: May the angel who redeems me from all evil bless the lads, and may my name be declared upon them, and the names of my forefathers Abraham and Isaac, and may they proliferate abundantly like fish within the land" (*Bereishis* 48:15-16).

Outsmarting The Enemy

Harav Yehoshua Dovid Povarski

Rosh Yeshivah,
Ponevizh Yeshivah

Outsmarting the Enemy

Harav Yehoshua Dovid Povarski zt"l, Rosh Yeshivah
*of the Ponevizh Yeshivah in Bnei Brak, was born in
5662/1902 in the town of Lubon, Russia. The noted*
Rosh Yeshivah *Harav Isser Zalman Meltzer discerned
Yehoshua Dovid's great potential and brought him to his
yeshivah in Slutzk immediately after his Bar Mitzvah.
The youngster's education was entrusted to Rav Isser
Zalman's illustrious son-in-law, Harav Aaron Kotler.*

*With the outbreak of World War I, Rav Dovid
joined the Mirrer Yeshivah in its exile in Poltava. It
was here that Rav Dovid developed his singular
attachment to the yeshivah's* Mashgiach, *Harav
Yerucham Levovitz, a closeness that lasted a lifetime.
Throughout the war he stayed with the Mirrer
Yeshivah in all its wanderings, until it returned to
its hometown of Mir.*

*After the war, he married the daughter of Harav
Dovid Dov Kreiser, one of the lecturers at the Kletzk
Yeshivah. That same year he published his first* sefer,
Yeshuas Dovid. *Later, he moved to Baranovitch and
studied together with its* Rosh Yeshivah, *Harav
Elchonon Wasserman. His reputation spread and he
received an invitation to join the staff of the noted
Yeshivah Chachmei Lublin. Rav Dovid spent several
weeks at the yeshivah and closely befriended its*

celebrated Rosh Yeshivah, *the Kozshligov Rav, author of* Eretz Tzvi. *Despite the prestige and financial security of the position in Lublin, he preferred to return to Baranovitch.*

With Divine Providence, he was successful in escaping the terrors of World War II and settled in Eretz Yisrael. *There, he was invited to serve as* Rosh Yeshivah *of the great Ponevizh Yeshivah, a position he held for over half a century. The* Rosh Yeshivah *merited longevity, passing away at close to 100 years old on 6 Adar, 5759/1999. During his long lifetime, he taught and guided thousands of worthy disciples who still carry the Torah torch of this great luminary today. His children follow in his footsteps, disseminating Torah in* Eretz Yisrael.

arav Yehoshua Dovid Povarski used to get up at 3:00 a.m. and walk over to the Ponevizh Yeshivah where he would learn Torah till the morning prayers. Nothing would hold him back from this routine, neither bitter cold nor sweltering heat; nor thunder and lightning; not even a high fever would stop him from his predawn Torah studies. Like a disciplined soldier in the royal guard, Rav Dovid stood at his post, studying for a four-hour, uninterrupted stretch.

In his later years, after he had slipped and fallen twice, his family became concerned for his safety and arranged for two of his best students to escort him. Once, during a very stormy, windy dawn, while walking to the yeshivah, Rav Dovid remarked to them that a special guest had come to him that morning: "*der Alter*" — "the old one." Since the title *Alter* — "Elder"— was generally conferred upon the spiritual mentors (*Mashgichim*) of the Lithuanian *yeshivos*, the students instinctively assumed that one of those saintly sages must have appeared to the *Rosh Yeshivah* in his dreams.

"Was it the *Alter* of Slobodka or the *Alter* of Kelm?" one of them queried, referring to the two most famous spiritual mentors in the prewar yeshivah world.

"Neither of them and not of their likes," the *Rosh Yeshivah* replied with a faint chuckle. "The *Alter* who visited me this morning was very old, I would even venture to say ancient; one who is thousands of years old, and whom the Sages have called 'an old stupid king,' the *yetzer hara* himself."

Continuing in the same vein, one of the students asked, "Isn't it strange that the *yetzer hara* did not find a more suitable prey than the *Rosh Yeshivah*? What did he think he could accomplish with his predawn visit?"

"Let me explain," the *Rosh Yeshivah* said. "Although he is described as stupid, the *yetzer hara's* early morning proposal seemed quite smart, like that of a highly experienced, cunning individual with a specific mission. He suggested that I stay in bed just five additional minutes, basing his proposal on a sound, logical premise: The entire world is now enjoying a sweet, relaxing sleep. Wouldn't it pay to invest just five minutes to satisfy the Sages' recommendation: 'Never detach yourself from the public'?

"I will confess to you," Rav Dovid said, "that his reasoning was quite compelling, and I actually began to consider his proposal in earnest. While I was contemplating the idea, the *Alter* again approached me. Using the same reasoning, he recommended that it might be more appropriate to remain in bed for not just five minutes, but for ten, perhaps fifteen minutes, with an open-ended option for an extension. Shouldn't the dictum 'Never detach yourself from the public' be carried out in the most comprehensive, thorough fashion?

"I immediately jumped out of bed with alacrity so as not to fall into his trap."

Turning to his students, the *Rosh Yeshivah* continued in a somber tone. "Throughout life a person is confronted with an ongoing battle with the *Alter*. The challenge is to succeed in the first five minutes. The victors are termed by the Sages as 'those of supreme strength.' Those who succumb during the critical first five minutes lose the battle."

Indeed, Rav Dovid was most conscientious not to fall prey to the "five-minute ruse." Once, upon arising in the morning, he was notified that there was a breakdown of the electrical system at the yeshivah, which shut down both the lighting and heating systems. He nonchalantly put on his coat and headed to the yeshivah as usual. His family tried to dissuade him, arguing that he would not be able to accomplish much sitting in the dark, freezing study hall.

Rav Dovid, though, was adamant. "I'd rather sit in the cold with no lighting and go on with my daily routine; for should I miss even one day, the next day it will be that much harder for me to arise. It is worthwhile for me to waste a day, as a bulwark against the instigations of the *yetzer hara*."

Needless to say, the *Rosh Yeshivah* did not waste any time at the yeshivah, utilizing every minute for a thorough oral review of many Torah subjects, despite the bitter cold that pierced through the bones of his frail body.

A Clever Prescription for Compassion

Harav Chaim Meir Hager

Vizhnitzer Rebbe

A Clever Prescription for Compassion

Harav Chaim Meir Hager zt"l, the Vizhnitzer Rebbe, was born in 5648/1888 in the town of Vizhnitz on the Galician-Romanian border. His father, the Ahavas Yisrael, was a scion of the Vizhnitz-Kosov dynasty and was descended from Harav Yaakov Koppel, one of the Baal Shem Tov's most respected disciples.

When he was only 17 years old, his scholarship and piety were well known and the Rachmistrivke Rebbe chose him as a suitable match for his daughter. He spent several years in his father-in-law's company and rose to great heights in Torah and Chassidus under his teaching and influence. After five years, he was selected as Rav of Vilchovitz in the Marmorosh region and strengthened Torah observance there greatly.

With his father's passing in 5697/1937, he relocated to the city of Grossvardein to fill the position as Vizhnitzer Rebbe. His amiable disposition and golden character attracted thousands of Chassidim who flocked to the city to seek his advice and blessing. He also established a large yeshivah, which existed until the outbreak of the war.

With the onset of World War II and the Nazi annihilation of Poland's Jews, he opened his house to the many refugees who were successful in escaping to Grossvardein. During this period, the Rebbe spent his entire time aiding the unfortunate refugees, seeking to alleviate their pain and suffering in every way possible.

In 5704/1944, the Nazis invaded Hungary and immediately decreed a series of anti-Jewish ordinances. The atmosphere became poisoned and anti-Semitic brutalities became the order of the day. Through a series of miracles, the Rebbe and his family escaped to Bucharest, Romania. Their intention was to immigrate to Eretz Yisrael, a goal that was realized only after several years. During his residence in Bucharest, the Rebbe injected a spirit of optimism into many spiritually emaciated souls who were affected by the ceaseless suffering and deprivation. The Rebbe, with his perpetual warmth and reassuring amiability, created a total transformation in the lives of these lost Jews, and brought many back to their tradition.

After the war, he returned to Grossvardein and reestablished his yeshivah. However, the Communists' rise to power changed his plans, and in 5707/1946 he made his way to Eretz Yisrael. Initially, he settled in Tel Aviv. His time there, however, was to be relatively short: he immediately began building Shikun Vizhnitz, a Vizhnitz community in the budding Chareidi town of Bnei Brak. He moved into the shikun in 5710/1950.

Over the years, he successfully established a wide array of religious and communal facilities within the shikun, including vast educational and chesed networks. Vizhnitz Chassidus began to sprout and branches opened in many Israeli cities as well as overseas.

Rav Chaim Meir passed away on 9 Nissan, 5732/1972. His children continue to lead the Vizhnitz communities in Eretz Yisrael and in America.

person once came to consult the Vizhnitzer Rebbe, Harav Chaim Meir Hager, about a friend of his, a Vizhnitzer Chassid who was afflicted with a dreadful, incurable disease. Apparently the patient had become totally demoralized from the treatments and the pain, and was refusing to take food and medications.

Reasoning with him was ineffectual. "There is no cure for my sickness, so why extend the agony?" he countered. "This is not a case of suicide; all I'm doing is refraining from eating. Nature will do the rest," he rationalized.

The Rebbe listened attentively to every detail and was obviously touched to the core. He related a series of stories from the Sages, all of which highlighted the phenomenal power of *emunah* and *bitachon*, faith and belief in *Hashem*, in repealing even the most devastating decrees. Instructing the visitor to convey them to his sick friend, he said, "The main thing is to emphasize and reemphasize that health and sickness are both in the hands of *Hashem*, and He is the only one who may decide on matters of life and death."

When the man was about to leave, the Rebbe turned to him and said, "Here is some practical advice on how to get those vital medications and foods into his system. Go immediately to the hospital and ask for details on the regimen prescribed for him. With this information in hand, go and visit your friend and tell him that you are just coming from seeing me. Tell him, 'When the Rebbe heard of your condition, he ordered that you take these medicines and eat these foods,' giving the impression that it all originated with me, not with the medical staff."

Then the Rebbe added, "I know what must be going through your mind. 'Is this really the Torah path? A Rebbe is teaching one of his closest followers to lie?' In a sense, you are right. The fact is that the very foundation of the Torah is *emes*, truthfulness, to the degree that our Sages tell us that *Hashem's* very stamp is *emes*.

"But your story touched me greatly and I am heartbroken over the man's condition. I am reminded of a story about Harav Boruch'l of Mezhubuzh, and my advice to you is in light of that story:

"A simpleton from Mezhubuzh derived his livelihood delivering goods from town to town. One day, while his wagon was loaded with merchandise, he entered a roadside inn and was tested with a major *nisoyon*, along the lines of the temptations confronting *Yosef HaTzaddik* in *parshas Vayigash*. He overpowered his *yetzer hara* and came away a true winner. The man was overwhelmed with joy. He was engulfed in a state of euphoria, almost losing touch with reality.

"In this state of excitement he left his horse and wagon — along with all the merchandise — parked in the town square, while he ran to his Rebbe, Rav Boruch'l Mezhubuzher, to share his happiness with him.

"The Rebbe happened to be sitting with his Chassidim and disciples, but the deliveryman was oblivious to his surroundings. He barged in and blurted out his remarkable story. Hearing the man's tale, and realizing that the man's wagon had been left unattended, the Rebbe raised his voice in a tone of deep anger and admonished the man. 'Have you abandoned other people's money? If, G-d forbid, the entire stock will be stolen, do you actually believe that you could absolve yourself from responsibility by relating your amazing experience? Run back immediately, fetch your wagon and save your customers' property.'

"The man was stirred back to reality. He rushed to town and, luckily, found his horse and wagon untouched.

"Rav Boruch'l then remarked to his listeners, 'I realize that you are surprised by my behavior. Within a couple of minutes, a simple man rises to exceptional spiritual heights, conquering the *yetzer hara* in a magnificent fashion. Instead of sharing the man's elation and crediting him for his exemplary behavior, I hollered at him and sent him running.

" 'Please be aware that it was not anger which I exhibited and it was not out of annoyance that I said what I said. I am also well aware of the great sin of insulting a fellow Jew. Yet, I felt that in order to save the man's source of livelihood and eliminate the heartache should the merchandise be stolen, the only avenue open to me was immediate, direct rebuke. If I should be punished with *Gehinom* for my behavior, I will accept it graciously. As a matter of fact, as far as I am concerned, I would more than welcome forfeiting my *Gan Eden* so long as a fellow *Yid* does not lose his income.' "

With this, the Vizhnitzer Rebbe concluded his message, remarking, "Although I realize my limitations compared to the holiness of Rav Boruch'l Mezhubuzher, I have learned a major lesson from his behavior. Regarding the present situation, if the most prudent way to persuade your friend concerning his diet and medications is through altering the facts, then that's the desirable path. A *Yid's* life supersedes all other considerations."

Grateful to the Plants

Harav Yisrael Zev Gustman

Rosh Yeshivah,
Yeshivah Netzach Yisroel

Grateful to the Plants

*Harav Yisrael Zev Gustman zt"l, Rosh Yeshivah
of Yeshivah Netzach Yisrael in Brooklyn, later in
Yerushalayim, was born in 5669/1909 in the town of
Vizhan, Lithuania. His father was Harav Avrohom Zvi,
one of the foremost disciples of the great Chofetz Chaim.
Even before his Bar Mitzvah, Yisrael Zev was sent to
study in the prestigious yeshivah of Harav Shimon Shkop
in Grodno. At age 16 he was appointed head of a
student's Talmud group whose members constituted the
elite of the yeshivah. The group included students who
would later become leaders in their own right: Harav
Shmuel Rosovski,* Rosh Yeshivah *of the Ponevizh
Yeshivah; Harav Eliyahu Mishkovski, founder of Yeshivah
Knesseth Chizkiyahu in Kfar Chassidim; and Harav
Naftali Wasserman, son of Harav Elchonon Wasserman.*

*When he was only 22 years old he was elected to
join the Rabbinical Court of Harav Chaim Ozer
Grodzinski in Vilna, the youngest member of this
august group in the city's history. He became a
favorite of Rav Chaim Ozer, who delegated many
challenging tasks to him, both domestic and those
relating to* Klal Yisrael. *We find him writing elaborate
responsa on behalf of Rav Chaim Ozer to some of the
greatest Torah sages of his generation, among them
the Tchebiner Rav, Harav Yechezkel Abramski and the*

Rebbes of Satmar and Gur — all before Rav Yisrael Zev even reached the age of 30.

During World War II he suffered indescribably. As he himself recounted, there were over one hundred occasions when death was so imminent that he actually recited Viduy. He spent lengthy periods of time as a member of the partisans, hiding in the forests and subsisting on shrubs and bushes. It was here that he witnessed the brutal murder of his only son הי"ד.

Broken in body but not in spirit, he arrived at the American shores and established a Talmudic institute named Netzach Yisroel, where he taught Torah to an elite body of students. In 5721/1961 he immigrated to Eretz Yisrael and transplanted his yeshivah to the Rechavia neighborhood of Yerushalayim. Many people from the general public joined the yeshivah students in attending his lectures, which gained distinction due to their clarity and intelligibility. It was said that upon hearing Harav Gustman's discourses on any Talmudic subject, it was almost impossible not to become proficient in the subject matter.

He passed away on 28 Sivan, 5751/1991. His son-in-law succeeded him in the post of Rosh Yeshivah.

Harav Yisrael Zev Gustman had a habit of personally watering the garden in front of his Yerushalayim yeshivah, which included a variety of plants, flowers and shrubbery. Although his students tried to dissuade him, noting that it was not becoming for the *Rosh Yeshivah* to indulge in work generally relegated to the maintenance crew, Rav Gustman insisted on watering the plants himself.

One of his close disciples approached Rav Gustman at an opportune moment and asked him why he was so adamant in performing manuel labor, especially in light of the fact that he never wasted a minute that could be used for the study of Torah or its dissemination.

"Let me explain," Rav Gustman said, with palpable emotion. "You are surely aware that before the war I served as a member of Harav Chaim Ozer Grodzinski's rabbinical court in Vilna. Our relationship was totally professional. We discussed rabbinical law or congregational matters, both local and worldwide. Many of our discussions and deliberations took place in the municipal botanical gardens of Vilna, situated adjacent to the Jewish community headquarters.

"One time, while discussing an important matter, Rav Chaim Ozer unexpectedly turned to me and began explaining the various plants and shrubs in the garden. He detailed their nutritious and medicinal value and identified which ones are dangerous to human touch or consumption.

"As a junior member of the court, I did not feel it appropriate to question this great sage as to what had motivated him to suddenly interject such an insignificant matter in our discussion.

"Years passed and the Holocaust overtook us. Like all European Jews, I found myself hounded and hunted down like a wild beast. For long periods of time I hid in the thicket of the forest, using the trees as my only shield against detection. How, you might wonder, did I sustain myself throughout this time? The answer is, the shrubbery and undergrowth of the trees were my only means of nourishment. Only then did I realize the Divine wisdom and prophetic perception of my great mentor, Rav Chaim Ozer, whose lessons in the basics of botany literally sustained me during those trying years.

"That is the reason I water the plants personally. It is my way of saying 'thank you,' of expressing my gratitude to them for having nourished me in time of need."

The Simple Things in Life

Harav
Yaakov
Leiser
Pshevorsker Rebbe

The Simple Things in Life

Harav Yaakov Leiser zt"l, the Pshevorsker Rebbe, fondly known as "Reb Yankele," was born in 5666/1906 in the Galician town of Roig. His father, Harav Dovid Yitzchak, was one of the elite Chassidim of the Shiniver Rebbe and served as Yaakov's full-time teacher during his formative years. He later wrote in a letter: "...my modest mother taught me Rashi; then I studied under my father, my master, Chumash and several hundred pages of Gemora, until I was 12."

At the age of 16 he became a follower of the Koloshitzer Rebbe, a great-grandson of the Sanzer Rebbe, the Divrei Chaim. For the next seventy-seven years, till Reb Yankele's passing, not a day passed without him mentioning either a dvar Torah or an educational anecdote from his beloved Rebbe.

In 5691/1931 he became engaged to the daughter of Harav Moshe Yitzchak Gewirtzman, commonly known as Reb Itzikl Pshevorsker. That same year he was also elected to the position of Rav in the town of Yashlisk. The engagement lasted four full years: the delay resulted from the fact that whenever Reb Itzikl accumulated any substantial sum toward wedding expenses, he always discovered some impoverished individual who seemed to need it more. The wedding finally took place in 5695/1935, and the couple came to live in Pshevorsk, in close proximity to the illustrious Reb Itzikl.

When the Second World War broke out, Reb Yankele was exiled to Siberia. Even in that dreadful, desolate land, subjected to slave labor under the domination of cruel, anti-Semitic overseers, he managed to observe every detail of halachah and minhagei Yisrael, sanctifying the name of Hashem on a lofty plateau.

After the liberation, he settled in Paris along with his father-in-law, and in 5717/1957 they moved to Antwerp. Wherever they resided, their first and foremost concern was to alleviate the needs of the poor and needy as well as performing the great mitzvah of hachnossas orchim — welcoming guests, transients and the homeless to their home.

After the passing of Reb Itzikl in 5737/1977, Reb Yankele was appointed to succeed him as Pshevorsker Rebbe. During the last twenty-two years of his life, throngs of people journeyed from all corners of the world to seek his advice and blessing and to search for inspiration in avodas Hashem. His house was open twenty-four hours a day: a skilled chef was hired to prepare elaborate meals for whoever may happen to enter and wished a delectable repast. His Chumash/Rashi lectures, as well as his tish — especially the weekly Melaveh Malkah Tish — inspired all those who attended.

He passed away at the age of 93 on 27 Cheshvan, 5759/1999. His son succeeded him as Pshevorsker Rebbe.

There is a story similar to Rav Gustman's told of Harav Yaakov Leiser, *zt"l*, who expressed appreciation even for the rough pebbles in his path:

Rav Leiser, known to all as Reb Yankele Pshevorsker, once went walking with a group of his Chassidim. The road was not paved; it was simply covered with a layer of pebbles, making walking quite uncomfortable. His disciples urged him to move to a parallel route, which was covered with a thick layer of fine grass. The Rebbe, however, adamantly refused.

The Chassidim were surprised, since the stroll was not intended to take the Rebbe to a specific destination; rather, it was to carry out his physician's orders to promote blood circulation. Why then should the Rebbe prefer the uneven, uncomfortable road of pebbles to the comfortable carpet of grass?

Noting their surprise, the Rebbe explained:

"There is a special reason why I prefer walking on the road of pebbles. I do this to express *hakoras hatov* — gratitude. When I was exiled to Siberia, a barren, underdeveloped, primitive land, the place where we lived and worked lacked any form of pavement. How terrible life was when the rain came pouring down! The entire area became one great swamp of mud, making the simple task of walking a major hurdle. Imagine our hardship in having to meet specific work quotas, chopping and shipping huge logs and lumber under these adverse conditions. In the rain, every step was an obstacle course.

"Eventually, the camp administration recognized that our production was hindered due to these monstrous mud swamps. Since it was in their own interest to enhance the road surface, they decided to cover the area with a sheet of pebbles. Words cannot express the joy and ecstasy we felt upon receiving this 'luxury.' For a long time we blessed *Hashem* daily for this great gift.

"It is because of this experience that I feel a special fondness for the pebbles which gave me and my fellow inmates so much joy. Utilizing them by treading on them allows me the opportunity to express my sincere gratitude for the simple things in life, which we all take for granted."

Guiding a Wayward Youth

Harav Avrohom Yeshayahu Karelitz

The Chazon Ish

Guiding a
Wayward Youth

Harav Avrohom Yeshayahu Karelitz zt"l, the "Chazon Ish," was born in 5639/1879 in the town of Kosova, Lithuania. His father, Harav Shmaryahu Yosef, served as Rav of the town. The boy became known for his diligence in Torah, his humility and his remarkable yiras Shomayim. On the day of his Bar Mitzvah he made a lifetime commitment, from which he never swayed, to learn Torah lishmah — only for the sake of pleasing Hashem, without the least ulterior motive.

In 5671/1911 he published his first work, Chazon Ish, Volume I, concealing his Hebrew name Avrohom Yeshayahu in the acronym ISH. His analytical sefer on the complicated tractate Kaylim was authored in those difficult days.

During World War I he was forced to escape to central Russia, and he settled in Vilna after the war. Despite his unusual humility and the fact that he did not occupy any official rabbinical post, he was recognized as one of the great Torah sages of Vilna — "The Jerusalem of Lithuania" — partly due to the extraordinary reverence accorded him by Harav Chaim Ozer Grodzinski.

In 5693/1933 he immigrated to Eretz Yisrael and settled in the budding Chareidi town of Bnei Brak. Here, too, he did not occupy any official post; yet, he exerted

*a profound influence on all segments of the population
— Chassidim, Lithuanians, Ashkenazim and Sephardim.
The Chazon Ish shared the happiness as well as the
sorrow of his brethren; his refined, self-sacrificing traits
were indeed exceptional. His prayers were an
emotional, spiritual outpouring of love to* Hashem.

*Throughout his life he would study Torah
unremittingly until he literally collapsed from
exhaustion. He would then nap a bit and return to his
studies. Over the years, he published a series of*
seforim *titled Chazon Ish, covering the entire
spectrum of Torah subjects, and was accepted as one
of the great halachic authorities of all time.*

*He guided an entire generation, accentuating
both orally and in writing the phenomenal bliss
experienced by those who dedicate themselves to
toiling in Torah. Indeed, large numbers of young
people followed in his footsteps and relinquished
life's comforts for the higher ideal of ascending the
ladder of* avodas Hashem.

*In his later years, his reputation was universal and
people flocked to his humble residence in Bnei Brak
from all corners of the earth to receive advice and
blessings from the* godol hador. *He received everyone
with exceptional warmth and helped the needy with
large sums of money, which were given to him by
admirers to be distributed to the poor.*

*The Chazon Ish passed away on 15 Cheshvan,
5714/1953. Although he was not blessed with children,
his* seforim, *his halachic decisions and his warm,
perceptive counseling — reflected in the published
volumes of his letters — are his everlasting memorial.*

During the early years of the Ponevizh Yeshivah in Bnei Brak, a new student was accepted who aspired to grow in Torah, yet he had also joined a non-*Chareidi* youth group. The group's entire outlook was poles apart from the yeshivah's. The matter was brought to the attention of the *Mashgiach*, the spiritual guide of the yeshivah, Harav Eliyahu Eliezer Dessler, who was very disturbed over the matter.

The *Mashgiach* spoke to him and tried explaining that just as light and darkness cannot operate jointly, similarly, one cannot ascend to high levels in Torah while participating in a youth club.

The student, however, was adamant that Torah study and the youth group were an ideal synthesis. The more the *Mashgiach* spoke to him, the more he became entrenched in his belief. Furthermore, he adopted the facade of a principled individual, publicizing his position to whoever was ready to listen.

The administration of the yeshivah tried impressing upon him that his behavior was viewed very seriously, and that the state of affairs could not continue any longer. Nevertheless, the lad was unyielding and he was finally requested to leave the yeshivah.

At that time there was a student at the yeshivah who later became known as Rav Shmuel Tzvi Kowalsky. When he learned that the boy was expelled from the yeshivah, he advised him to visit Rav Avrohom Yeshayahu Karelitz, better known as the Chazon Ish. The Kowalsky boy briefed the Chazon Ish, who then had a heart-to-heart discussion with the boy, encouraging him greatly to strive to become a real *ben Torah*. He also advised him to apply to the Lomza Yeshivah in Petach Tikvah and he gave him a letter of recommendation to expedite his acceptance.

In private, the Chazon Ish also advised Shmuel Tzvi that when the *Rosh Yeshivah* of the Lomza Yeshivah would try to test his friend, he should preempt the answers and respond correctly to the questions.

The two youngsters arrived in Petach Tikvah and presented themselves to the *Rosh Yeshivah*, Harav Yechiel Mechel Gordon. He welcomed them with his usual warmth, and was especially friendly after he read the personal letter of the Chazon Ish.

Rav Gordon began to test the boy, presenting him with a challenging question on his most recent studies at the Ponevizh Yeshivah. And here the spectacle began to unfold. The *Rosh Yeshivah* asked a question and the Kowalsky *bachur* interceded with an answer. The *Rosh Yeshivah* asked another question, directing it squarely at the other boy, but Kowalsky answered it. It did not take long for Rav Gordon to catch on to the scheme. Notwithstanding the comical scenario, the boy was accepted. Apparently, the crucial letter of the Chazon Ish worked wonders.

After a short time, however, the old problem began to resurface. Evidently, when the boy moved to Petach Tikvah, he took along his alter ego, the *yetzer hara*, who joined him at the Lomza Yeshivah. Following a brief acclimation period, the boy found his way to the local branch of his favorite youth club.

Needless to say, the administration of the yeshivah was vehemently opposed to this and tried to dissuade him, but they encountered a wall of resistence. Two weeks later, when Shmuel Tzvi visited the yeshivah, the situation had deteriorated, seemingly beyond help.

He proposed that they again visit the Chazon Ish, and the boy readily agreed. Upon their arrival, Shmuel Tzvi first went in alone and briefed the Chazon Ish on the latest developments, emphasizing that the original problem had resurfaced and that there was a distinct possibility that the boy would be expelled from this yeshivah as well. He respectfully asked that the Chazon Ish give the boy a harsh rebuke, stressing to him how detrimental his lifestyle was to his spiritual growth.

When the boy came in, the Chazon Ish welcomed him with fatherly love, displaying a keen interest in every phase of his life, especially in his educational progress. He asked him to relate a Torah elucidation he learned from his *rebbes*. The boy was greatly impressed with the interest bestowed upon him and felt a keen sense of pride in the close relationship he seemed to have developed with the *godol hador* — the greatest Torah sage of the generation. The Chazon Ish then invited him to return the following week so that he could relate some of his own Torah insights.

After leaving the house, the boy rushed back to Petach Tikvah to share his experiences with his classmates and to begin an intensive learning program in preparation for his upcoming visit with the Chazon Ish. He ardently wanted to present his own *chidushei Torah*.

After the boy had left, the Kowalsky boy mustered the courage to question the Chazon Ish about the total absence of any reprimand. This is what the Chazon Ish replied:

"It is obvious that this boy derives great pleasure from his membership in the club. It is impossible to remove something from a person without replacing it with something of similar value. Needless to say, Torah has all the ingredients of eternal pleasure and bliss, unparalleled by any worldly activity. However, the boy has not yet reached that level of spiritual sophistication to fully appreciate it; his eyes have not yet opened sufficiently. I've invited him for the coming week, hoping that in the interim he will immerse himself in Torah study, and in due time, when he will experience the true flavor of Torah, all his childish desires will fall by the wayside."

As the Chazon Ish predicted, the boy began a regimen of intense Torah study, experiencing a spiritual satisfaction he had never felt before. About two weeks later, the boy lost his most devoted, intimate friend, his great mentor and guide, the Chazon Ish. However, his profound influence remained ingrained in his heart forever: No more youth groups, no more social clubs. What filled the boy's spiritual vacuum was delving into Torah, growing in *avodas Hashem* and discovering the perpetual kinship between man and his Creator. Today, the hero of our story is one of the outstanding Torah scholars in the great city of Bnei Brak.

A Grandfather's Confident Hope

Harav
Moshe
Aaron
Stern

Mashgiach, Kamenitz Yeshivah

A Grandfather's Confident Hope

Harav Moshe Aaron Stern zt"l, Mashgiach of Yeshivah Kamenitz in Yerushalayim, was born in New York in 5686/1926. His father was Rav Yom Tov Lipman, and his mother, Esther, was the daughter of Rav Yaakov Yosef Herman (the subject of Ruchoma Shain's book, All for the Boss), *who was called the "Chofetz Chaim of America" by Rav Boruch Ber Leibowitz. In his youth, Moshe Aaron studied in Yeshivah Torah Vodaath as a dedicated disciple of its illustrious founder, Rav Shraga Feivel Mendlowitz. He was one of a core of pioneer students who were ready to dedicate their lives to Torah, even in the materialistic American society of those days.*

At the age of 18, he went to Palestine to study in the Kamenitz Yeshivah of Yerushalayim, a difficult task during the British Mandate era. After marrying into one of Yerushalayim's most distinguished families — that of Reb Chaim Yosef Kreuzer — he began lecturing at the yeshivah, and eventually became its Mashgiach. His mussar sermons penetrated deeply into the hearts of his students, who appreciated the fact that he was a living testimony to the lofty ideals he taught.

In addition to his official duties at the yeshivah, Rav Moshe Aaron dedicated his life to the needs of others. Hundreds of people from several continents benefited from his advice and counsel. The verse "I am with the despondent and lowly of spirit" (Yeshayahu *57:15), is most descriptive of Rav Moshe Aaron's outlook, as he was a caring confidant to the deprived and the dejected.*

As a native New Yorker fluent in the English language, he was sent overseas twice yearly to help raise funds for the yeshivah. *Even during his travels, he focused on helping others, especially in the field of* shalom bayis, *bringing harmony to families in distress. One of the great* Roshei Yeshivah *aptly defined Rav Moshe Aaron as fulfilling the role of* **Moshe** Rabbeinu — *the master teacher of* Hashem's *Torah — while at the same time serving as* **Aaron** HaKohen — *the great symbol of peace-loving mediation. It is noteworthy that only three days before his passing, Rav Moshe Aaron delivered a major address at a girls' academy, encouraging the students to continue in the paths of the matriarchs.*

He passed away on 8 Adar, 5758/1998. Inspired by their father, his children are known for their Torah and chesed *in Israel and America.*

It was the custom of Harav Moshe Aaron Stern to visit his granddaughters during their hospitalization in the maternity ward and bring them an assortment of delicacies and refreshments, in addition to a special gift — an outfit for the newborn baby.

Indeed, this was a bit unusual, since it is generally the parents or grandmother who bring sets of clothing, not the grandfather. Even the nurses commented admiringly about this extraordinarily thoughtful grandfather.

One time, Rav Moshe Aaron came to visit a granddaughter who had finally given birth, after many years of marriage. As expected, the proud grandfather arrived with his parcel of gifts. After greeting her with a heartfelt *mazal tov*, he opened his suitcase and handed her a pink outfit for her baby girl. While the mother examined the gift with appreciation, the grandfather brought out another set and then yet another set of clothing for her baby, emptying the contents of his valise.

Upon scanning the entire array of gifts, the cheerful mother turned to her grandfather and asked, "Zaidy, I hope you realize that I gave birth to only one baby, not a set of quintuplets! Why did you bring this entire collection for my one little girl?"

"Let me explain," he said tenderly. "As you know, since I am an American, the Kamenitz Yeshivah has chosen me to travel overseas twice yearly. Prior to returning, I make sure to buy sets of clothing for all my grandchildren. Throughout the years, while shopping for these gifts, I felt that you should not be left out just because you were not yet blessed with offspring. So I always made sure to shop for your future children. Not knowing if you will have a boy or a girl, I bought clothing for both. The contents of this valise are the 'she' gifts accumulated throughout the years. *Im yirtzeh Hashem*, at the right time, the suitcase of 'he' gifts will follow."

The Z'chus of Torah Lishmah

Harav
Yosef Zvi
Dushinsky

Rav of Yerushalayim

The Z'chus of
Torah Lishmah

*Harav Yosef Zvi Dushinsky zt"l, Rav of the Eida
HaChareidis in Yerushalayim, was born in Paksh,
Slovakia in 5627/1887. His father, Harav Yisrael, was
a disciple of the Maharam Schick, one of the most
distinguished students of the Chasam Sofer. At the age
of 11, he studied at the yeshivah of Harav Moshe Falk
in Bonyhad, Hungary. His diligence in Torah was so
intense that upon becoming Bar Mitzvah he refused to
return home, forgoing any celebrations or ceremony, so
as not to lose time from his studies. His* Rosh Yeshivah,
*however, insisted that he relate some original Torah
thought for the special occasion. Acquiescing to his
rebbe's wishes, the boy lectured on a complex
Talmudic theme that encompassed many important
and intricate subjects, all prepared on his own.*

*He continued his studies in Pressburg, studying
under the tutelage of the Shevet Sofer. Despite his
tender age, he was considered among the elite in this
most prestigious yeshivah with an enrollment of over
four hundred students. His reputation spread, and
Harav Mordechai Winkler, Rav of the city of Maad
(author of the famous works* Levushei Mordechai*),
chose him as his son-in-law.*

In 5655/1895 he was elected as Rav of Galanta,
Slovakia, and immediately established a yeshivah. As

*Harav Dushinsky quickly gained a reputation as one
of the most gifted* Roshei Yeshivah *in the country,
students flocked to his yeshivah from Slovakia and
Hungary. Throughout his life he kept to a rigorous
regimen, delivering an average of three Torah lectures
daily. In 5682/1922 he ascended to the rabbinate of
the prominent city of Chust. Here, his yeshivah
expanded greatly, enrolling hundreds of students.*

Harav Yosef Zvi visited Eretz Yisrael *in 5692/1932.
During his stay, the venerable* Rav *of Yerushalayim,
Harav Yosef Chaim Sonnenfeld, passed away.
Following the funeral, Yerushalayim's elite visited
Harav Dushinsky stating that they recognized the
Divine Providence in their late* Rav's *words alluding
to Rav Yosef Zvi remaining in Yerushalayim. He was
placed at the helm of leadership.*

During the seventeen years he served as Rav *of
the Holy City, he led his flock with understanding
and wit. He established an educational system
encompassing all levels from kindergarten through
postgraduate. He fought with fierce determination in
defense of the sanctity of Yerushalayim, especially
regarding Sabbath observance.*

*Harav Yosef Zvi passed away on 14 Tishrei,
5709/1948. The leadership of the yeshivah and its
accompanying institutions was placed on his son,
who eventually rose to his father's prominent position
as* Rav *of Yerushalayim.*

During World War I, many Jews evaded military service in
the Polish army. Due to rampant anti-Semitism in the
armed services, even those inducted absconded at the
first opportunity. The closest haven was Hungary, and many of

the escapees found their way to the Galanta Yeshivah. These young men were longing to continue their Torah studies. Despite their physical and psychological hardships, living in an alien land and subject to arrest and deportation, they dedicated themselves with gusto to their studies. At the time, the yeshivah was headed by the illustrious Harav Yosef Zvi Dushinsky, who also served as *Rav* of the city. Years later, he was elected to the prestigious position of *Rav* of Yerushalayim.

One day, the military police made an unexpected foray into the yeshivah's district in search of undocumented aliens hiding in the city. News of the operation did not reach the yeshivah in time. Suddenly, while the *Rosh Yeshivah* was in the middle of his lecture, the school was surrounded by soldiers, headed by a high-ranking officer. A shudder went though the spines of the Polish students, for upon arrest they would immediately be extradited to their homeland, where long prison sentences, perhaps even the death penalty, awaited them.

The foreign boys instinctively ran for cover, attempting to jump out of windows, hoping to escape via the courtyard. But this option was also closed, as the entire building was surrounded.

The *Rosh Yeshivah* motioned to everyone to return to his seat. His cool style and self-confident manner calmed them somewhat, and the lecture continued as before. After several minutes, the officer entered the *beis medrash* and announced that he came in search of illegal aliens.

Words cannot describe the panic and anguish of the Polish students as they realized that there was no escape. Yet, the *Rosh Yeshivah's* demeanor was strangely incongruous to their state of mind. Even at this critical point, his calm did not leave him, as if he were oblivious to the impending crisis.

Suddenly, the *Rosh Yeshivah* turned to the students, pointing out the Polish citizens one by one and ordering them to line up. It became crystal clear, even among the bravest of the group, who until then had maintained a semblance of composure, that Rav Dushinsky was not ready to sacrifice the entire yeshivah for a few Polish aliens. Apparently, the *Rosh Yeshivah* had come to the conclusion that each of these boys would be considered what the *halachah* terms *rodeph*, a person about to cause death to another person. The *halachah* specifies that in such cases one may save the victim, even by causing death to the *rodeph*.

After they lined up, the *Rosh Yeshivah* turned to the commanding officer and declared: "I wish to point out that these young men whom I've ordered to line up are longtime students at the seminary. I know each of them on a personal basis; they are all loyal Hungarian citizens and your honor does not need to bother establishing their documentation. However, those remaining seated include some new students and I cannot personally vouch for them."

The *Rosh Yeshivah's* deportment, along with his absolute command of the situation, impressed the officer greatly and it did not dawn on him to challenge the "facts." Upon examining the documents of the "new" students who had remained seated, he was satisfied that everything was in order and the soldiers left on a friendly note.

Only then did the Polish boys breathe a sigh of relief. Everyone sensed that what had occured was, in fact, what the *mishnah (braissa)* in *Pirkei Avos* alludes to with the statement, "Everyone learning Torah *lishmah* [for the sole objective of serving *Hashem*] is *zocheh* to many things ... and it gives him kingship and governing powers [leadership qualities of the highest caliber]."

A fascinating postscript: Following this incident, the yeshivah never again was visited by any law enforcement agents. In fact, not one of the hundreds of yeshivah boys in the city was ever stopped, even for a routine ID inspection, throughout the entire four-year period of the war.

Shlomo's Wisdom

Harav
Avrohom
Shlomo
Katz

Rav of Riskeve

Shlomo's Wisdom

Harav Avrohom Shlomo Katz zt"l, the Riskever Rav, was the son of Harav Eliyahu, Rav of Raslavitza, one of the foremost specialists in the field of halachic arbitration of monetary disputes. In his youth, Avrohom Shlomo studied in Chust in the yeshivah of the Arugas HaBosem, who ordained him. Following his marriage to the daughter of Harav Zvi Bergfeld, Rav of Nimiza, he relocated there. Like his father, he became an expert on Choshen Mishpat, *the Code of Jewish law dealing with financial matters. He was also ordained by the Darkei Teshuvah of Munkacs; the Zichron Yehudah of Satmar; and the world-renowned* Rav *of Radimishla, Harav Shmuel Engel.*

When Rav Avrohom Shlomo's father-in-law passed away in 5675/1915, he was chosen to fill the position. During the post-World War I era, he gained fame through his outstanding expertise on the subject of agunos *-- finding halachically valid ways to allow women whose husbands were missing to be classified as widows and thus allowed to remarry. In 5684/1924 he ascended to the post of* Rav *of Riskeve. In addition to performing rabbinic functions and arbitrating disputes in his rabbinical court, he established a yeshivah that came to be considered one of the great Talmudic centers of the Hungary/Romania region.*

During this period he also published his classic sefer, *Orchos HaMishpotim.*

When World War II broke out, the city of Riskeve was within Hungarian territory. The anti-Semitic Hungarian regime decreed that all foreign-born citizens be expelled immediately from the country. This law, while seemingly reasonable in wartime, was in actuality a death sentence for Jews from Poland. Jews were being annihilated there on a massive scale. Rav Avrohom Shlomo managed to escape to Budapest, where he evaded the Nazis by hiding in a bunker.

After the war, he returned to Romania and established a highly regarded community in Klausenburg, as well as a yeshivah for Holocaust survivors. His experience from the post-World War I era prepared him to play an active role in resolving problems of agunos, *which was perhaps the most pressing issue of the day. Together with the venerable Harav Chaim Mordechai Roler, Rav of Niamtza, he toiled unremittingly to find halachic solutions to these grave problems.*

When the Communists took power in Romania he immigrated to the West, first to France and then to America. Immediately upon setting foot in the United States, the Satmar Rebbe incorporated him into many of his activities toward the strengthening of Yiddishkeit. *He was also among the founders of the Central Rabbinical Congress of the United States and Canada, commonly known as Hisachdus HaRabbanim. The Riskever Rav was a skilled orator, known for his great integrity: over the years, he became a respected spokesman for the* Chareidi *viewpoint.*

In 5722/1962, despite his advanced age of close to 80, he was appointed as Rav *of Kiryas Yoel in Bnei Brak. Here, as in all of his rabbinic posts throughout his career, his numerous talents were brought to bear in the establishment of a dedicated Torah lifestyle among his constituents, the Satmar community of Bnei Brak.*

He passed away on 14 Nissan, 5735/1975, leaving behind a generation of Torah scholars. His son filled his rabbinical position in Bnei Brak.

During Harav Avrohom Shlomo Katz's tenure as *Rav* of Nimiza, Romania, prior to assuming the prestigious rabbinical position of Riskeve, an incident took place that publicly highlighted his intelligence and perceptiveness.

A youth from one of the towns near Nimiza entered into a business venture and in the process befriended many of the town's gentiles. He once traveled on business to Klausenburg together with a gentile friend and the gentile's wife. With darkness approaching, they stopped at a roadside inn and rented two rooms, one for the young man and the other for the couple.

They awoke at sunrise to resume their travels, but upon checking his belongings, the gentile realized that his wallet with all his money was missing. Needless to say, the most obvious suspect was the Jewish lad. The police were summoned and they arrested the youth. Only after intensive intervention by the Jewish community leaders was he released until the trial date.

With such great misfortune befalling him, the boy was desperate for advice and help, and he turned to Rav Avrohom Shlomo for assistance. The *Rav* listened attentively to his account, and harshly chastised him for his permissive attitude in traveling in the company of a gentile and his wife, which is not only contrary to *halachah* [Rambam's *hilchos rotzeiach ushmiras nefesh* 12:7] but is also contrary to minimum moral standards. The youth was sincerely remorseful and promised to mend his ways by allocating significant periods of time for Torah study.

Upon examining all facets of the story, the *Rav* was convinced of the boy's integrity regarding the missing money, and came up with an innovative approach to proving his innocence.

He suggested that the lad propose to the gentile that he take the case out of the civil legal system and have the matter arbitrated by the *Rav*. In doing so, the matter would be resolved speedily and at minimum cost to the parties involved. As far as objectivity is concerned, he suggested that the gentile make inquiries among his friends to ascertain that a truly fair trial would be held in the *Rav's* rabbinical court. After a few days, the gentile came back with a positive reply, and a date was set for a meeting in the rabbi's chambers.

The gentile presented his case and, as expected, the boy denied the claim that he had stolen the money. After intensive cross-examination, the *Rav* handed down his verdict that the lad must take a religious oath that he is innocent of the theft.

The swearing session was scheduled to take place in the main synagogue and in the presence of all interested parties. When the appointed day came, the synagogue was fully packed with spectators, Jews and gentiles who came *en masse* to observe the scene. The women's gallery was also filled to capacity, including the gentile's wife.

A deathly silence permeated the sanctuary as the *shammos* lit large black candles, removed a Torah scroll from the ark and placed it into the *Rav's* hands. The *Rav* turned to the youth and addressed him in a forceful voice: "Pay heed, that within a few short minutes you will take hold of this Torah scroll and swear in the name of *Hashem* that you did not lay a hand on the missing wallet and its contents.

"Our Torah stipulates dreadful repercussions for oaths of this magnitude. Should you swear falsely, terrible curses shall befall you — diseases, poverty and misfortunes — followed by a terrible death. On the other hand, should you be innocent, then the oath you will be taking will cause all of these misfortunes to rest on the head of the actual perpetrator of the crime."

The youth approached the *Rav* and with trembling hands was about to clutch the Torah, when suddenly loud shrieks echoed from the women's gallery. A woman was screeching, "Stop, stop! For Heaven's sake, don't swear!"

All eyes and ears turned upward to the origin of the commotion. The woman became hysterical. "I beg you not to swear," she wailed. "I promise to return the entire amount I stole from my husband, but for Heaven's sake, don't swear! Don't bring death and misfortune upon me!"

The *Rav's* brilliant plan had worked.

Simchas Chosson and Kallah

Harav Shraga Feivel Mendlowitz

Menahel,
Mesifta Torah Vodaath

Simchas Chosson and Kallah

Harav Shraga Feivel Mendlowitz zt"l, Rosh Yeshivah of Mesivta Torah Vodaath in Brooklyn, New York was born in the town of Vilag, on the Hungarian-Galician border in the year 5657/1897. His mother passed away when he was only 10, and subsequently his father moved to Rimanov, Galicia. As a student in the yeshivah of Harav Moshe Grunwald in Chust, he excelled in his studies to the degree that prior to each shiur Rav Moshe inquired whether Shraga Feivel was present: "Without him, I just can't conduct my lecture." His rebbe entrusted him with editing his classic sefer, Arugas Habosem.

Rav Shraga Feivel continued his studies in Unsdorf, under the leadership of its acclaimed Rosh Yeshivah, Harav Shmuel Rosenberg, one of the primary marbitzei Torah in Hungary. Here he went through most sugyos haShas in great depth, as well as the entire Yad HaChazakah of the Rambam and all four volumes of the Tur with Beis Yosef. Prior to his departure from the yeshivah at age 18, his rebbe granted him rabbinical ordination. He continued his studies in Pressburg, under the tutelage of Harav Simcha Bunim Sofer, son of the renowned Ksav Sofer.

In 5673/1913 he immigrated to America and settled in Scranton, Pennsylvania. He tried his luck in business, but was unsuccessful. He became a Hebrew teacher in the local Talmud Torah, where he mesmerized his students with his phenomenal educational talents. His reputation traveled far and wide, and he was invited to head Yeshivah Torah Vodaath in Brooklyn, New York, the most prestigious yeshivah of that era. Rav Shraga Feivel thrust himself with zest and passion into his new position, and after a short while was successful in establishing Mesivta Torah Vodaath, one of the first post-elementary Orthodox Jewish schools in America. His charisma, coupled with his dedication to establishing limud haTorah *in a land where this was an alien value, helped him reach success. It is largely to his credit that a new generation of American-born young men, devoted completely to* Yiddishkeit, *galvanized to form the core of a Torah renaissance in America.*

Rav Shraga Feivel was never complacent, never satisfied with past accomplishments. When barely finished with the monumental task of establishing the Mesivta he immediately went to the next logical step — to set up a post high school Talmudic center: Bais Medrosh Elyon, in Monsey, New York was styled after the great yeshivos of Eastern Europe and provided a kollel *for married students to continue their postgraduate rabbinic studies.*

Toward the end of his life, while a debilitating terminal sickness gnawed at his body, Rav Shraga Feivel bolstered himself with superhuman energy and established the vital educational organization Torah Umesorah, a network of Hebrew day schools throughout America. In the course of time, this organization has grown to be one of the foremost institutions of American Jewish life, embracing over a quarter of a million students.

Rav Shraga Feivel's extraordinary success can be attributed to his selfless dedication to Hashem, without any ulterior motives. Recognition and honor were totally alien to him and were fought off with a passion. He went so far as to insist that he not be addressed by any rabbinical title, but preferred to be known simply as Mr. Mendlowitz. How aptly the Ponevizh Rav commented: "Rav Shraga Feivel is not a Mister; rather, he is a nistar" (an extraordinarily virtuous and pious man, hiding under the cloak of simplicity). Harav Aaron Kotler once commented that were it not for Rav Shraga Feivel, Torah would never have flourished in America.

He passed away on 3 Elul, 5708/1948 and was brought to his final resting place in the plot of the Ponevizh Yeshivah in Bnei Brak, the city of Torah that he had helped to build. He left a large family dedicated to the dissemination of Torah in America and in Israel.

Harav Shraga Feivel Mendlowitz will be remembered for posterity as the "father of the yeshivah movement of America." He rightfully earned this designation, for in the short span of approximately twenty years he successfully built a Torah empire of colossal proportions. A builder of such caliber is often focused on the "big picture," lacking the time and mental resources to care about individuals — but not Harav Mendlowitz.

We can catch a small glimpse into the mindset of this giant — whose heart overflowed with infinite love for each and every one of his students — from the following letter, written while he was recuperating from a severe heart attack in Liberty, New York. In it, he regrets that he is unable to physically participate in a student's wedding:

My dear and beloved, who is engraved within the depths of my heart,

I think it is superfluous to describe to you my profound yearning to participate and share with you this happiest moment of your life. It will be no exaggeration to say that for a long time I waited with a rare sense of anticipation for this propitious occasion. My mind's eye has been carrying me to the wonderful opportunity to partake in the dances and merrymaking at your wedding. Alas, "Many designs are in man's heart, but only the counsel of Hashem *prevails."*

However, please note, my dear friend, that only my body, with its three-dimensional confines, will stand from afar. My soul and spirit, which transcend the limits of time and space — the true "I" which is inseparably bound to your soul — will, with Hashem's *help, actively take part in your day of rejoicing. I conclude with my sincerest blessings…*

With a heart of this magnitude, it is small wonder that he accomplished what had been thought impossible — the renaissance of Torah on North American shores.

Similarly, once during World War II, Reb Shraga Feivel attended a meeting of the Vaad Hatzolah, a rescue organization. The meeting dealt with the horrible conditions in the ghettos and concentration camps. Listening to reports of the incredible pain, suffering and wanton murder of his fellow brethren, Reb Shraga Feivel cried uncontrollably.

From the meeting, he proceeded directly to the wedding reception of one of his students. He greeted the *chosson* pleasantly, wishing him *mazal tov* and the customary good wishes. Despite Reb Shraga Feivel's attempts to camouflage his distraught state of mind, the *chosson* easily sensed it. He approached his *rebbe* and asked: "Haven't you always told me that the sky would be the limit to your joy and happiness at my wedding?"

Instantaneously, Reb Shraga Feivel's demeanor changed dramatically. He literally burst out in song and danced with unparalleled enthusiasm. To him, honoring a promise, even if it had been stated hyperbolically, overrode all other considerations.

A Parallel Experience

A student studying at Mesifta Tiferes Yerushalayim was faced with an awkward situation. He was a *chosson*, and as his wedding day approached, he realized that he would not be able to offer his beloved *Rosh Yeshivah*, Rav Moshe Feinstein, any honors at the wedding.

"I must ask the *Rosh Yeshivah* for forgiveness. Both my bride and I are from distinguished rabbinical families, so all the customary honors have been assigned to close family members."

Listening to the apology, Reb Moshe smiled and said: "Put your mind at ease. It is no problem at all. It will be my pleasure to attend your wedding without being accorded any honors. With the help of *Hashem*, I will participate and join in the dancing at your *simchah*."

True to his word, Reb Moshe graced the wedding with his presence. As scheduled, an array of prominent rabbis, all close relatives of the *chosson* and *kallah*, received the honors under the *chupah*, leaving no *brachah* for Reb Moshe.

After the ceremony, Reb Moshe extended his cordial, heartfelt blessing to the *chosson* and *kallah* and to their families, wishing them *nachas* and bliss. He then departed for home.

Back at the hall, the wedding proceeded with its festive meal and joyous dancing. Some three hours into the dinner, the guests were in for a most pleasant surprise: Reb Moshe was back! He approached the *chosson* with his characteristic warmth and explained: "When we last spoke at the yeshivah about your upcoming wedding, I had expressed my intention to attend your *simchah*. After I returned home, it occurred to me that I had also mentioned joining in the *dancing* as well." The *Rosh Yeshivah* proceeded to participate in a joyous dance, returning home at a late hour.

Such precision in keeping his word was in line with Reb Moshe's lifelong emphasis on emulating the Creator, Whose very seal is engraved with the word "*Emes*" — Truth.

The Greatest Z'chus

Harav Shlomo Zalman Auerbach

*Rosh Yeshivah,
Yeshivah Kol Torah*

The Greatest
Z'chus

Harav Shlomo Zalman Auerbach zt"l, Rosh Yeshivah *of Yeshivah Kol Torah in Yerushalayim (born 5670/1910), was the son of Harav Yehuda Leib, founder of Yeshivas HaMekubalim Shaar HaShamayim in Yerushalayim.*

During his student years at Yeshivah Etz Chaim he became known as a great illuy *(prodigy) and was very beloved by its illustrious* Rosh Yeshivah, *Harav Isser Zalman Meltzer. At only 22 years of age he authored a penetrating book on the* shev shmaatesa, *and three years later he enthralled the Torah community with his book,* Meorei Hoeish, *on the status of electricity on Shabbos. Even the great* Rav *of Vilna, Harav Chaim Ozer Grodzinski, sent his approbation praising the young author.*

His reputation spread throughout Eretz Yisrael *and several rabbinical posts were offered to him. Rav Shlomo Zalman finally consented to head Yeshivah Kol Torah, where he disseminated Torah for scores of years and was* zocheh *to guide thousands of worthy students. Many of his students have subsequently taken positions as rabbis and Roshei Yeshiva of rabbinical schools in Israel and the Diaspora.*

As the years progressed, his halachic decisions were widely accepted and Rav Shlomo Zalman

*became known as one of the most eminent Torah
authorities. Dozens of his analyses were printed
in Torah journals and quoted in the works of
contemporary authors. Over the years, he published*
Maadanei Melech *on the laws of* shviis *and* terumos.
Thousands of copies of his book Minchas Shlomo
*have been distributed and it has become a standard
for the entire Torah community.*

*He passed away 19 Adar I, 5755/1995. The
funeral procession was one of the biggest of all
time, with hundreds of thousands in attendance
— men, women and children — all bemoaning
the loss of this mighty beacon of Torah light. His
children are renowned Torah leaders who continue
in his footsteps.*

A young widow came to seek the advice of Harav Shlomo
Zalman Auerbach regarding a matter that weighed heavily
on her heart. Her husband had passed away at a young
age, leaving her a widow with four young orphans.

"Please help me," she said with an expression of deep
anxiety. "My conscience is tormenting me. Days and nights I
agonize over the possibility that I did not care sufficiently for my
husband during his illness. I'm convinced that had I done more,
I could have prevented the tragedy. I feel that perhaps I can make
it up to him by taking on a *mitzvah* for the sake of his *neshomah*.
I have come to you for guidance as to what specifically I should
undertake in order to give him a special *z'chus*."

"Your decision is indeed most commendable," said Rav
Shlomo Zalman. "*Chazal* state: '*broh mezakeh abba* — a child
has the ability to affect *z'chuyos* for his deceased father'. I will

direct you on a course that will accomplish this purpose. Please pursue the following three-pronged program:

"First, as soon as you leave my house, go directly to a toy store and buy the children toys and games; don't stint on the cost. Second, make it a habit to take the children on trips and outings to places they enjoy. Finally, try your best to overcome your feelings of grief, especially in the presence of the children. Concentrate instead on creating a happy home environment.

"Always bear in mind," Rav Shlomo Zalman concluded, "that happy children do better in school, behave better at home and are more successful in all their endeavors. If you stick to these guidelines, the children will, with *Hashem's* help, grow up to be thriving, Torah-true Jews. Indeed, this is the greatest *z'chus* that you can bestow upon your late husband."

Ever Scrupulous in Truthfulness

Harav Yehuda Tzadka

Rosh Yeshivah,
Yeshivat Porat Yosef

Ever Scrupulous in Truthfulness

*Harav Yehuda Tzadka zt"l, Rosh Yeshivah of Yeshivat
Porat Yosef, was born in Yerushalayim in 5668/1908.
His father, Harav Shaul, was a descendant of Harav
Tzadka Chutzin. On his mother's side he was a
grandnephew of the renowned Ben Ish Chai and
descended from Harav Abdullah Somech. He studied
under Harav Ezra Atyah, founder and* Rosh Yeshivah *of
Yeshivat Porat Yosef in the Old City of Yerushalayim,
eventually the most prestigious Sephardic Talmudic
institute in the world. Another of his mentors, Harav
Yaakov Addas, recognized his extraordinary faculties
and fine character and groomed him for leadership.*

After years of diligent study in the kollel *of Yeshivat
Porat Yosef, he was appointed at age 24 to join the staff
as a lecturer. Nearly thirty-eight years later, following
the passing of Rav Atyah in 5730/1970, he was
appointed* Rosh Yeshivah *of the yeshivah. Aside from
his phenomenal knowledge of all phases of Torah,
including Kaballah, he was admired for his noble traits
and sensitivity to others. Above all, he was noted for
his supreme humility. In his role as* Rosh Yeshivah, *Rav
Yehuda inspired his many students with his
illuminating insights on the complexities of Torah,
shaped the unique identity of the yeshivah and carried
the budgetary responsibility of the school.*

*In the last decade of his life, Rav Yehuda Tzadka's
name spread throughout* Chareidi *Jewry and he was
considered one of the generation's eminent Torah
sages. He set the tone for dozens of institutions,
primarily Sephardic; and a large share of the
renaissance of Torah among Sephardic youth can be
attributed to him. Two years before his passing, he
published his* sefer, Kol Yehuda, *which is a masterpiece
in its field. It contains but a small fraction of his
extensive manuscripts.*

*He passed away on 12 Cheshvan, 5752/1991,
leaving behind a distinguished family of Torah
scholars, as well as thousands of students who occupy
rabbinical and leadership positions in Israel, America,
France and Latin America.*

A student at Yeshivat Porat Yosef in Yerushalayim was tested by Harav Yehuda Tzadka on the *Shulchan Aruch* (Code of Jewish Law) pertaining to the sections customarily studied toward *semichah*, rabbinical ordination. The student passed the examination satisfactorily, and also demonstrated proficiency in many Talmudic themes.

Rav Yehuda was ready to issue him the standard rabbinic degree and advised the young man to visit a certain scribe who served as the yeshivah's *sofer* to write and personalize the document. The student returned the following day for the *Rosh Yeshivah's* signature.

As per custom, all ordination certificates bore the signatures of two of the yeshivah's foremost Roshei Yeshivah. In his humility, Rav Yehuda suggested that the student should first have Harav Benzion Abba Shaul, an associate *Rosh Yeshivah*, sign it and he would follow suit. The student visited Rav Shaul, who graciously signed. The next morning he returned to Rav Yehuda, but to his dismay, the *Rosh Yeshivah* glanced at the document fleetingly, and refused to sign it.

"Pardon me a thousand times for all the inconvenience I am putting you through," Rav Yehuda said, "however, I am sorry to tell you that I cannot sign a document which is not wholly truthful.

"Hopefully, you will one day serve as a rabbi — a shepherd of G-d's flock. In the very first chapter of *Shulchan Aruch, Choshen Mishpat* (the section of the Code dealing with monetary matters), the *Tur* quotes the *Gemora:*

'כל דיין שדן דין אמת לאמיתה נעשה שותף להקב"ה במעשה בראשית.'

— 'Every rabbinical judge who adjudicates law in a true/truthful manner becomes a partner with Hashem in the Creation.' As you surely note, the expression אמת לאמיתה 'true/truthful,' seems redundant. But in fact, it's not. It is stated twice — as though it were appearing in bold letters — for a specific reason: namely, to accentuate the primary importance we place on the rabbi's honesty.

"Upon closer scrutiny, you will note that the date appearing on the certificate is incorrect. The text reads: 'Written and signed this 26th day in the month of Av, in the year...,' when in reality, today is already the 27th day of Av." To reinforce the concept of adhering to absolute truth, Rav Yehuda related a very similar anecdote about Harav Ezra Atyah.

"A student once approached Harav Atyah to obtain his signature on an important proclamation issued by many of the sages of Yerushalayim. The incident took place years ago, when Yeshivat Porat Yosef was still in the Old City, in close proximity to the *Kotel HaMaaravi*. However, the meeting between Rav Ezra and the student was held in the New City. While reviewing the document, Rav Ezra noticed that the last line read: 'We, the undersigned, here in the Old City of Yerushalayim...' Noticing that line, he refused to sign the document, as it did not reflect the truth: at that moment they happened to be in the New City. However, in view of the urgency of the matter, Rav Ezra put on his overcoat and said to the student, 'Let's go to the Old City, for the sake of אמת לאמיתה, absolute truth. There, I will sign the document, and we can then return immediately.'"

Rav Yehuda Tzadka's student fully appreciated his *rebbe's* reservations in signing his ordination. In those short minutes, he gained a wealth of practical rabbinical experience, as our Sages state "גדול שימושה יותר מלימודה", "Attending to a Torah sage is often more beneficial than studying Torah from him." He returned to the scribe who changed the date. He then resubmitted it to his *rebbe*, who welcomed him with great warmth, signed the certificate and wished him great success in his future role as a *manhig eidah b'Yisrael* — a rabbinical leader in Israel.

In Zealous Defense of Torah

Harav
Shlomo
Goldman

Zviller Rebbe

In Zealous
Defense of Torah

Harav Shlomo Goldman zt"l, the Zviller Rebbe, was born in 5630/1870. His father was Harav Mordechai, a direct descendent of Harav Mechele Zlotchiver. When his father passed away in 5660/1900, the burden of leadership fell on Reb Shlomo's shoulders. He did not hesitate to wage battle with the various antireligious Zionist and Bundist groups that proliferated in those tumultuous days.

After the Bolshevik Revolution, he continued his leadership despite strict anti-Jewish laws and succeeded in establishing a network of religious institutions including an exemplary Talmud Torah.

In 5686/1926 he immigrated to Eretz Yisrael. *Before the ship anchored, he asked his grandson who had accompanied him not to divulge his identity to anyone because, in his words, "I wish to serve* Hashem *in the Holy Land as a simple person without the trappings of honor and respect associated with leadership." Upon arrival in Yerushalayim, he lived with paupers and the homeless — the most down-trodden population of the Holy City. For years, the* Rav *of Yerushalayim received sums of money by mail earmarked for "the Zviller Rebbe," but the money had to be put in safekeeping, as the* Rav *could not locate anyone by that title throughout the city.*

After a number of years, a man from Zvill happened to visit the Chayei Olam Yeshivah and noticed a pauper sitting in the far corner of the room, studying ceaselessly. As he approached the poor man, he instantly recognized him to be none other than the Zviller Rebbe. An uproar ensued throughout the city: the Zviller Rebbe had been found! Realizing that he could no longer live in anonymity, he reassumed the mantle of the rabbinate as in days past. Despite the constant demands on his time, the Rebbe devoted himself totally to the needs of the orphans and the homeless, whom he had come to know through his years of living incognito, and he established appropriate quarters for them in his own house.

Throughout the bitter years of the Holocaust he beseeched Hashem with prayers and tears, begging for his grief-stricken brothers and sisters in the European inferno as well as for the Jewish community in Eretz Yisrael. *The very day of the allies' victory in Europe (26 Iyar, 5705/1945), Reb Shlomka fulfilled his mission on earth and returned his soul to his Creator. His son carried on the leadership of the Zvill community.*

Harav Shlomo Goldman, the Zviller Rebbe fondly known as Rav Shlomka Zviller, led his flock in the town of Zvill for a quarter century, nine years of which were under Communist rule. Immediately following their victory, the Bolsheviks decreed ruthless edicts against all forms of religious practice, with a particular vengeance against all aspects of *Yiddishkeit.*

A special group of Jewish Communists, known as the *Yevsektzia* (literally "Jewish Section"), was given the mandate to uproot all expressions of Judaism. Its members were assimilated, self-hating Jews. They closed synagogues, Talmud Torahs and *mikvaos*, and hounded rabbis and *dayanim* aggressively. Most of the persecuted were exiled to the Siberian gulags or "disappeared" into the unknown. Despite these dreadful conditions, Rav Shlomka continued his sacred mission, maintaining a complete range of religious and educational services.

His *cheder* was underground; the *mikvah* was camouflaged; and all other religious services were provided under cover, constantly subject to the danger of discovery by the dreaded *Yevsektzia* which often worked with the secret police and local officials. When word was received that the secret police were in the area, *cheder* students would run to hide in the underground shelter, which was specifically set up for that purpose. When an official would enter the house, he would find no trace of a school and would have to leave without incriminating evidence.

Through the years, there were occasional incidents when members of the *Yevsektzia* would appear suddenly, catching the *cheder* unprepared. Somehow, despite their vitriolic hatred of religious Jewry, Rav Shlomka's very countenance seemed to mollify their feelings and change their plans. They repeatedly looked away from his "crime."

But the day of reckoning did arrive. One day, a Russian officer entered the house and was met by Rav Gedaliah Moshe, the Rebbe's son (and ultimate successor). After properly identifying himself with his military credentials, the officer went straight to the point, asking if an illegal Jewish school was being maintained on the premises — a school that indoctrinates its young students with the "cancer of civilization" [Karl Marx's notorious description of religion]. Rav Gedaliah Moshe turned white, confronted by the man's manifest anti-Semitism. He fully perceived the implications of the visit: it would result in the closure of the Talmud Torah and the banishment of his beloved father to Siberia.

Upon entering the room, the Rebbe noticed his son's anguished expression, and inquired about the officer's mission.

Rav Gedaliah Moshe explained that he came regarding the Talmud Torah, and that the situation was critical.

Rav Shlomka began screaming, as though attacked by a wild beast. "What? They want to close the Talmud Torah?" In his rage, he impulsively rushed to the officer, placing his hands around his neck and tightening his grip, as if he were ready to choke him.

Everyone in the house was frozen in disbelief, unable to utter a word, fearful of the consequences of this brazen act. Even in a democratic country, an act of this sort would be construed as attempted murder: all the more so in a Russian dictatorship when the victim is an army officer carrying out his official duties.

After a few seconds that seemed like an eternity, Rav Gedaliah Moshe came back to his senses and pleaded with his father to release his grip. Rav Shlomka acquiesced and the officer ran off in a state of fury.

Anguished weeks passed in the Rebbe's household. The only question was: How soon would the long hand of the law catch up with them? Ironically, the only one who seemed oblivious to the danger, not manifesting the slightest degree of anxiety, was Rav Shlomka himself. He continued all of his previous activities on behalf of the community, including the maintenance of his beloved Talmud Torah, despite his family's dire predictions and protestations.

Surprisingly, no negative results followed. None of the civilian or military law enforcement agencies pursued the affair, and the officer never surfaced again in Zvill. It was as if the earth had consumed him like Korach and his followers.

Throughout his life, Rav Shlomka refrained from discussing this miraculous affair. His family, however, felt that it was a *mitzvah* to publicize it so that others could appreciate the magnitude of a *tzaddik's* determination and fortitude in pursuing *Hashem's* Torah against all odds, even in the face of dreadful repercussions.

An Inspiring Precedent

A story from an earlier period has come down to us that demonstrates a similar selflessness in defending the study of Torah from those who would destroy it:

One of Harav Chaim Soloveitchik's *rebbes* in Brisk was Harav Dovid Blinder (Yiddish for "blind person"). Actually, Rav Dovid had perfect vision and was called *blinder* for an altogether different reason. A pious man, Rav Dovid was scrupulous not to tarnish the spirituality of his eyesight by looking at licentious sights. Instead, he turned his focus downward, giving the impression that he was blind.

Our story takes place in one of the darkest periods in Jewish history, the era of the cantonists. During this time, Jewish children in czarist Russia were kidnapped and handed over to the government to serve in the armed services for a span of twenty-five years. Since the story revolves around the cantonists, some background on the subject is necessary. We will then return to the story of Rav Dovid Blinder.

In the year 5605/1845 Czar Nikolai I decreed that five of every thousand Jews must be delivered by the Jewish community leaders to the government for service in the armed services. On the surface, it would seem like a reasonable law. In reality, however, it was the cruelest and most inhumane law ever enacted by the brutal Russian government.

This was not a draft decree in its conventional sense. Rather, even 5- and 6-year-old Jewish children were taken — essentially kidnapped — and delivered to peasants in distant rural areas who were responsible for their schooling. Their specific objective was to prepare the children emotionally and culturally for the rigors of army duty. Upon reaching 18, they entered the armed services for a period of twenty-five years.

The draft period was set to take place once every two years in the months of Kislev-Teves (December-January). Since the requirement was upon the Jewish community at large and not on each individual family, it is only natural that whoever had the opportunity to hide their children from the "snatchers" did so. At the end of the draft period, the children were taken out of hiding and were relatively safe for the next two years.

Since implementation of the law was the responsibility of the community and many categories of the population were legally exempt (such as licensed tradesmen and people considered vital to governmental interests), in essence it was mostly the very poor and downtrodden who bore the burden of supplying the requisite number of children.

The snatchers, accompanied by armed police burst into the homes of the destitute and kidnapped tender children from their mothers' laps. The children were lead to detention centers — armored, jail-like fortresses — to await delivery to the appropriate governmental agency. The sobs of the unfortunate parents whose darling little boys were snatched away from them were heart wrenching. Mothers gathered in front of the detention centers for weeks on end, ripping out their hair in anguish and wailing incessantly. Some lost their minds at the thought of the horrors awaiting their children.

During the training period, the children were entrusted to the custody of barbaric, anti-Semitic peasants who brutalized them with beatings and tortures in an attempt to force them to eat *treif* and desecrate the Sabbath. The goal of the process was to remove them from their Jewish upbringing and convert them to Christianity. The slightest violation of their edicts resulted in corporal punishment so severe that often the children bled profusely, developing severe sores from the beatings. Many died during their term of "training." It is for this reason that the months of draft turned into periods of deep sorrow, with no *simchos* taking place throughout the Jewish community.

We will now return to Rav Dovid Blinder:

During one of these draft periods, when the fear of kidnappings was on the minds of everyone, tens of thousands of young Jewish boys left their *chadorim*, descending into underground shelters to evade the snatchers. Rav Dovid's students also became accustomed to this practice. Needless to say, the militia's enforcement division did not sit idle either, but lurked persistently to fulfill the required governmental quota.

One day, while Rav Dovid was learning with his pupils, one of whom was the illustrious Reb Chaim Brisker (Soloveitchik), a police agent burst into the house and caught the entire group in the middle of learning. He grabbed one child and began dragging him outside, so that he could fill his quota.

The children were awestruck, totally helpless in the face of such unprovoked aggression against a defenseless classmate. Then suddenly, Rav Dovid got up from his chair, went straight to the police officer and slapped him on his cheek with all his might. The officer released the child and fled.

Under standard procedure, Rav Dovid would have been arrested immediately and kept in custody until his trial. In the interim, as per Russia's tradition of "justice," the detainee would be tortured and brutalized. Upon being judged guilty, he would be sentenced to hard labor in one of Russia's notorious gulags. This time, however, the entire incident was somehow silenced — and no arrest was made!

Rav Chaim Brisker's father, the famous "Beis HaLevi," once asked Rav Dovid, "How did you develop such courage and fearlessness, to slap a Russian police officer?"

"Believe me, *rebbe*, I did not do that with great planning or courage. We were engaged in a most complicated *Tosfos*. In comes this *orail* and disturbs us. What nerve, what *chutzpah*! Right in the middle of *Rabbeinu Taam's* explanation of a complex subject, when I was on the verge of getting through to my students, this wicked *goy* comes and disturbs us all. I slapped him for his impudence more than for anything else," Rav Dovid concluded.

Decades later, a young man arrived at the Chofetz Chaim's house in Radin, requesting admission to the yeshivah. In the course of conversation, the boy mentioned that he was a grandson of Rav Dovid Blinder. The Chofetz Chaim was very touched by the mere memory of Rav Dovid, and immediately waived all entrance requirements in deference to the boy's grandfather. He added a heartfelt *brachah* that the *z'chus* of his grandfather's *"mesiras nefesh slap"* should merit the boy great success in Torah and *yiras Shomayim*, following in his grandfather's footsteps.

Kiddush Over Hot Tears

Harav
Yona
Furst

Mashgiach, Nitra Yeshivah

Kiddush Over Hot Tears

Harav Yona Furst zt"l, Mashgiach of the Nitra Yeshivah in Mount Kisco, was born in 5676/1916 in Vienna. At an early age he was sent to study in the yeshivah of Harav Shmuel Dovid Ungar, Rabbi of Tirnau who later ascended to the rabbinate of Nitra, Slovakia. He advanced greatly in his studies and in piety; and with a thorough proficiency of hundreds of pages of Gemora, he was accepted by the prestigious Yeshivah Chachmei Lublin, headed by its illustrious founder, Harav Meir Shapiro, Chief Rabbi of Lublin.

While in Lublin, he contracted polio, a dreadful disease that paralyzed both of his legs. Due to his handicap, he returned to Nitra. There, he immersed himself totally in the sea of Talmud, napping in his wheelchair most nights instead of retiring to the dormitory. With the outbreak of World War II, he was expelled together with all foreign citizens across the border of Slovakia. Through the intervention of the Nitra Rav and his son-in-law, Harav Michael Ber Weissmandl, he was returned home to Nitra. Late in 1944, the Jewish population of Nitra was deported to the Auschwitz extermination camp, and Rav Yona was miraculously saved.

After the war, he returned to Slovakia and from there he came to America together with the Nitra

Yeshivah's faculty and students. The yeshivah was successfully rebuilt in Mount Kisco, a distant suburb of New York City, and he was appointed Mashgiach of the yeshivah. His influence transcended the confines of the school; it encompassed all segments of Orthodox Jewry. He attended countless meetings and assemblies on behalf of furthering Torah education and helped establish the profile of a Torah Jew in the United States.

More than anything else, he was always available to individuals to ameliorate their woes, solve their problems and inject a spirit of optimism into broken hearts, especially for the many postwar widows, widowers and orphans. He found the time and patience for lengthy counseling sessions necessary to restore peace and harmony into dozens of homes where marriages would have ended in divorce if not for his empathy and wisdom.

Rav Yona passed away on 16 Teves, 5743/1983. As he had no children of his own, he raised several "sons" who follow his example, disseminating Torah on a large scale.

It is appropriate at this juncture to dedicate a perpetual memory to one of Rav Yona's "sons": Harav Shlomo Feldman zt"l, who passed away at a young age. While supporting himself with a seforim store, he utilized every possible moment for Torah and yiras Shomayim. His aim in life was to instill love of Hashem and love for His Torah into the hearts of the young. Toward this objective, he established Talmud Torah Tiferes Yona, named after Reb Yona Furst.

This was not a Talmud Torah in the conventional sense. Rather, it was a meeting place for yeshivah children during after-school hours, as well as during vacation, "off" days and on chol hamoed. Often

hundreds of children gathered at the Talmud Torah,
where Rav Shlomo taught them love of Hashem and
helped them develop good character traits.

The children instinctively sensed that under the
guise of simplicity was a man who was a true tzaddik
and they formed a close, loving relationship with
him. Even during the years when he was afflicted
with a dreadful terminal disease, Rav Shlomo did not
relax his efforts; and with his last ounce of strength he
continued, even expanded, his activities on behalf of
"his children." He returned his soul to his Creator on
20 Tamuz, 5755/1995, leaving behind a wonderful
family who continue in his admirable ways.

One of the great educators of post-World War II America was Harav Yona Furst. As a teenager he was afflicted with polio, resulting in an incurable paralysis of the legs, and throughout his life he was forced to move about in a wheelchair. Despite this major handicap, or perhaps thanks to it, he overcame all obstacles and established a reputation as one of the most prominent spiritual advisers of Orthodox Jewry.

In many of his public appearances, Rav Yona elaborated on specific incidents of the Holocaust, highlighting the great lessons to be learned from them for gaining strength from misfortune. This is one anecdote he related during the days of *Selichos*, in preparation for the Days of Awe:

"It happened on Rosh Hashanah eve, 1945, in the infamous Theresienstadt concentration camp. A group of Jews had gathered secretly to participate in the prayers. They all were risking their lives, knowing well that at any moment a *kapo* might spot them, and the consequences would be severe, brutal beatings. [*Kapos* were overseers appointed by the Nazis to supervise the inmates and draw out their last pint of blood by enforcing their sadistic regulations.]

"It is not hard to imagine the outpouring of emotions at this prayer session. People who only a short time earlier had spent their holidays in the company of their loved ones were now standing in the shadow of death. There is no doubt in my mind that their heartfelt prayers burst open the gates of Heaven. At the conclusion of the service, the *chazzan* led the 'congregation' in a recitation of the traditional psalm, *'LeDovid Mizmor.'* If throughout the general service the emotional outpouring was visible, the ecstatic ardor was beyond description when they reached the passage: 'Raise up your heads, O gates ... so that the King of Glory may enter.' The entire congregation's yearning that shortly the King of Glory would open the gates of freedom was almost palpable.

"Following the service, one of the participants turned to the entire assembly with the question, 'And what about *Kiddush*?'

"His fellow prisoners stared at him with disbelief. Even contemplating wine for *Kiddush* in Theresienstadt was like trying to fly to the moon. What could the man possibly have had in mind when he asked about *Kiddush*?

"Listen attentively and you will appreciate the spiritual wellsprings which lie dormant within the soul of every *Yid*," continued Rav Yona. "Even at the gates of death, these people did not lose their G-dly image. What's more, they even rose from within their afflictions, as the prophet Yechezkel states: 'I say to you, with the spilling of your blood, you will come to life.' [16:6]

"The questioner took out a cup and said 'I suggest we make *Kiddush* — a *Kiddush Shem Shomayim* — a public sanctification of G-d's Name, the likes of which the world has never witnessed in its entire history. Let us make *Kiddush* on a commodity that is perhaps dearest to us, yet is available in great quantities, even in this dungeon. Since we do not have wine, let us substitute our tears. We all know that tears have a special ability to break through even iron barriers, as asserted in the *Ne'ilah* prayer:

יהי רצון מלפניך שומע קול בכיות
May it be Your will, He Who listens to the voice of weeping
שתשים דמעותינו בנודך להיות
That You place our tears in Your jug to be preserved
ותצילנו מכל גזרות אכזריות
And deliver us from torturous decrees
כי לך לבד ענינו תלויות.
For to You alone our eyes are turned.

"He placed the cup in the middle of the room and within moments it was filled to the top with the hot tears of the unfortunate Jews. He then raised his voice and began chanting melodiously the traditional Rosh Hashanah *Kiddush* 'אשר בחר בנו מכל עם ורוממנו מכל לשון וקדשנו במצוותיו.' — You have chosen us from among all nations, lifted us from among all tongues, and sanctified us with Your commandments.'

"It is indeed difficult for a mortal to envision the deep pride and holiness that permeated each of us at that moment. We were filled with the conviction that despite the beatings and suffering at every step and at every turn, we were still *Hashem's* darling children, the Chosen People whom He lifted from among the nations and sanctified with a heavenly holiness unparalleled by any other nation."

Rav Yona's words left a profound impact on his listeners, inspiring them to turn to *Hashem*, heart and soul.

The Precocious Philanthropist

Harav
Yoel
Teitelbaum
Satmar Rav

The Precocious
Philanthropist

Harav Yoel Teitelbaum zt"l, the Satmar Rebbe, was born in 5647/1887. His father, Harav Chananya Yom Tov Lipa, author of Kedushas Yom Tov, *was the Rav of Sighet. His grandfather was the Yetev Lev, who was in turn the grandson of the Yismach Moshe, founder of the Sighet/Satmar dynasty. At the age of 23 he was chosen as* Rav of Orshiva and from there *he moved on to Krula. In 5693/1933 he was chosen to head the rabbinate of Satmar, one of the foremost Jewish cities in Hungarian Romania. In every city where he served as* Rav, *his first order of business was to establish a yeshivah and to implement major improvements in the spiritual life of the city, specifically in the areas of* shechitah, tznius *and* shiurei Torah.

By the time he became the Satmar Rav, *he was renowned as a great Torah sage and as a singularly pious personage. Thousands from throughout Hungary and Romania flocked to him to seek his expert and insightful counsel. He was recognized as the leader of Transylvanian Jewry and as one of the outstanding* Roshei Yeshivah *whose yeshivah produced thousands of fine students.*

When the Nazis invaded Hungary he was exiled to the Klausenburg Ghetto. Through a special deal made with the Nazis, more than 1,500 Jews who had been temporarily held in the Bergen Belsen concentration camp were taken by train to freedom in Switzerland. The Satmar Rebbe was on that train.

Thus on 21 Kislev 5705/1945 he escaped from the horrors of the Holocaust. From there, he moved to Eretz Yisrael and immediately began establishing Torah and chesed institutions. After a year, he relocated to the United States.

Upon his arrival in America, he planned the building of a community along the lines of the prewar kehillah system in Europe. In that context, he built a huge independent school system, a kashrus apparatus, a major rabbinical organization and rabbinical courts, as well as a wide range of charitable and self-help organizations. In only thirty years, he successfully established an all-encompassing Chassidic culture with tens of thousands of adherents. Throughout his life he fought against all forms of Zionism with a passion. He authored two seforim on that subject: VaYoel Moshe and Al HaGeulah v'al HaTemurah.

In 5711/1951 he was chosen as Chief Rabbi of the Eida HaChareidis in Yerushalayim. Among the major institutions he established in America are the Central Rabbinical Congress of the U.S. and Canada (Hisachdus HaRabbanim); Keren Hatzalah — a special fund supporting Torah institutions in Eretz Yisrael that refrain from benefiting from government funds; and Rav Tov — an organization geared to helping immigrants and Jews facing persecution worldwide.

The Rebbe's prayers, especially during the Yomim Noraim and Hoshana Rabbah, "split the skies." His sermons and lectures stirred all with their powerful style and brilliance.

Branches of Satmar — with all their varied
educational and social activities — were established
in Orthodox population centers in Eretz Yisrael, the
U.S., Canada, Western Europe, Australia, and even in
small communities of South America. The Rebbe also
established a living example of a beautiful Yiddishe
shtetl, a Chassidic town in a distant New York suburb
that is named after him: Kiryas Joel.

The Satmar Rebbe passed away on 26 Av,
5739/1979 and was brought to his eternal resting
place in Kiryas Joel. Tens of thousands visit his
gravesite on the day of the yahrzeit. Among the
seforim he authored are Divrei Yoel on Torah;
Chidushei Sugyos; and Divrei Yoel Responsa. As he
did not leave any offspring, his nephew was chosen
as leader of the Satmar community.

The Kedushas Yom Tov appointed one of his most gifted Chassidim, Rav Yaakov Zvi, to supervise the spiritual development of his very talented nine-year-old son (who later became known as Harav Yoel Teitelbaum, the Satmar Rebbe). Indeed, the tutor lived up to the challenge, realizing that Yoilish'l, the youngster in his care, was of a totally different breed, one who had the potential to illuminate the entire Torah world.

Because of the frigid climate, the child's mother bought him a fur coat and asked Rav Yaakov Zvi to make sure he did not lose or misplace it because it was quite expensive. One day, the tutor realized that for the past several days the child was not wearing the coat and questioned him about it. Yoilish'l tried to evade the question, claiming that it was too cumbersome for him to put on the coat and reasoning that the distance from his house to the *cheder* was very short.

The excuses sounded a bit suspicious, and the tutor insisted that he wanted to know the exact whereabouts of the coat. Not having a way out, the child admitted that the coat was not presently in his possession: he had used it as collateral to secure a large loan of several thousand krona (the local paper currency) from one of the wealthy townspeople, a Chassid of his father! To Rav Yaakov Zvi, the story sounded preposterous. First, why does a young child need to borrow such a huge sum, and how will he repay it? Has the child turned into a businessman, offering his fur coat as collateral? In addition, why would a seasoned businessman place his trust in a little boy? True, Yoilish'l was not just another child; he was in a class of his own, both in terms of intelligence and piety. But after all, a child is a child!

At the first opportunity, Rav Yaakov Zvi visited the lender who corroborated the child's story, adding that on previous occasions Yoilish'l had borrowed small sums from him. He also related that the child always insisted on handing over his fur coat as collateral, and that his repayment record was exemplary. As far as the purpose of the loan was concerned, the man acknowledged that he had never asked him outright, but that he got the distinct impression that the loans were intended to help financially distressed people. That is the reason he was ready to accommodate the youngster, for he also wanted to participate in the *mitzvah*.

At this point, Rav Yaakov Zvi's curiosity was deeply aroused and he hurried over to Yoilish'l to learn the details of this most bizarre relationship.

"I'll tell you," Yoilish'l said with a shy smile. "A short while ago, a Chassid came to my father's study to discuss some private matter. I was in the adjoining room and my ears inadvertently picked up his heartbroken sobs as he told his story: The unfortunate man has a daughter who, after many years, finally became engaged to a fine man. The father undertook financial obligations to be paid prior to the wedding. That day was fast approaching and the man was desperate, for should he fail to come up with the money, the engagement would be broken.

"Although my father gave him a substantial sum, it was far from his enormous needs. On his way out, I asked the man to wait a bit and allow me to do something for him. I rushed to the house of a wealthy man and borrowed the money, leaving my fur coat as security. He was very gracious in extending the loan, and I immediately delivered the money to the father of the kallah.

"You have no idea, Rav Yaakov Zvi, how much joy I brought into the life of this poor man," the child concluded, with a sense of deep satisfaction over the great mitzvah he had carried out.

"But Yoilish'l dear, what about the fur coat? You know that your mother is quite worried about your health, and should she find out that you walk around without a coat during these freezing winter days she will be very upset with both you and me."

"I have a suggestion," said Yoilish'l with his angelic smile. "Let's be partners in the mitzvah. Between Minchah and Maariv we will approach all the congregants in shul. The Sages have guaranteed us that Klal Yisrael is a holy nation and always responds favorably when asked, because charity is part of our very essence. Once we receive the first donation, the others will come easily, since mitzvah goreres mitzvah [performing one mitzvah creates a spiritual atmosphere allowing for more mitzvos to be performed]. There will be a built-in bonus too — the mitzvah of kibud ame [honoring one's mother], for the sooner I repay the debt, the faster I will retrieve my coat."

That very day, a most unusual team approached the congregants: a well-respected, learned, middle-aged man and an adorable little boy, soliciting donations for hachnossas kallah.

While they were going from congregant to congregant, the Kedushas Yom Tov spotted them and inquired about their mission. Rav Yaakov Zvi briefed him on the story. The father was visibly moved and inspired by his little son's outstanding sensitivity to the pain of a fellow Jew and by his adult sense of responsibility. To encourage him to do similar undertakings in the future, he contributed a most generous sum, far above his means. By day's end, the entire amount was collected. In addition to the great *mitzvah* of *hachnossas kallah*, Yoilish'l also performed the fifth of the Ten Commandments in a splendid way, and his frail body received a well-deserved gift: his warm fur coat.

A Unique Siyum HaShas

Harav Zelig Reuven Bengis

Rav of Yerushalayim

A Unique
Siyum HaShas

*Harav Zelig Reuven Bengis zt"l, Chief Rabbi of
Yerushalayim, was born in 5624/1864 in a suburb of
Vilna. His father was Harav Zvi Hirsch. By the age of
10, Zelig Reuven was well known for his excellent
scholarship. The youngster's abilities became nearly
legendary during a visit of the Ridvaz, when he
engaged the great sage in a masterful Talmudic debate.*

*At the age of 17, he was accepted into the
Volozhin Yeshivah, a prestigious rabbinical school.
The* rosh yeshivah *of the yeshivah, the Netziv,
predicted that the lad would become one of the
leaders of* Klal Yisrael. *Throughout his years at the
Volozhin Yeshivah, his learning partner was the
future great sage Harav Isser Zalman Meltzer. Their
friendship spanned more than seventy years, first in
Lithuania and later in Yerushalayim. Harav Chaim Zvi
Broyde, president of the Union of Lithuanian Rabbis,
chose Rav Zelig Reuven as his son-in-law. For many
years after his marriage the young man studied under
Rav Broyde's tutelage, becoming proficient in all
aspects of Jewish law.*

In 5654/1894 he became the Rav of Budki, a
*suburb of Brisk, and served there for close to twenty
years. From there he ascended to the prestigious
position of* Rav of Kalbaria *and served the needs of that*

community for over a quarter century. In 5698/1938 he immigrated to Eretz Yisrael *and was appointed head of the Rabbinical Court of the Eida HaChareidis in Yerushalayim. After the passing of Harav Yosef Zvi Dushinsky, he was named Chief Rabbi of the Holy City.*

He passed away 2 Sivan, 5713/1953. His classic six-volume Liflagos Reuven *earned him a highly respected standing for posterity.*

Harav Zelig Reuven Bengis was known for his supreme diligence in Torah study, even by the high standards of the Holy City of Jerusalem. Every few months, he invited a group of friends and associates to celebrate a *Siyum HaShas*, the completion of study of the entire Talmud. These repasts were modest in nature, both in their arrangement and menu. Generally, only bread, herring and some whiskey to make a "*l'chaim*" were served. The *Rav* would say the *hadran*, followed by *Kaddish*, and offer a brief Torah insight. After about five or six months, the same routine would be repeated.

One time, about a month after the previous *Siyum HaShas*, the *Rav* again invited his customary attendees to celebrate the completion of the entire *Shas*. The invitation surprised everyone, as it would have been impossible even for Rav Zelig Reuven to accomplish such a feat in such a short time. What was even more surprising was the relative elegance of the table settings and diversified menu prepared for the affair. Everyone washed and sat down to the meal, eagerly waiting for some clue as to the meaning of it all. To be sure, the explanation was not long in coming.

"Let me explain the nature of this *siyum*," the *Rav* said with obvious emotion. "From the time that I assumed the post of *Rav* of Yerushalayim, I made a firm decision that I would make every effort to arrive on time to all social affairs, so as not to cause undue inconvenience to anyone in attendance. I adopted the practice of arriving several minutes before the scheduled affair was to take place.

"From the very first *simchah* I attended, I made it a habit to use the few minutes before the affair for an extracurricular master-review of the entire Talmud, in addition to my routine review of *Shas*. Today, after years of attending hundreds, perhaps thousands of affairs, the extra minutes have accumulated into untold hours, and have translated into thousands of pages of *Gemora*. This is the reason I have gone to the expense and effort to create a truly special atmosphere for this celebration. To finally complete the entire *Shas*, a few precious moments at a time, is a major highlight of my life."

The Power of a Good Name

Harav
Avrohom
Weinberg
Slonimer Rebbe

The Power of a Good Name

Harav Avrohom Weinberg zt"l, the Slonimer Rebbe, was born in 5649/1889 in Eretz Yisrael. *Although his father, Harav Noach, originally had been from the town of Slonim, Poland, he had been sent by his father (the Yesod HoAvodah) to* Eretz Yisrael *in 5630/1870, before his Bar Mitzvah. At the time, the Yesod HoAvodah said that a terrible cloud of darkness someday will engulf European Jewry; therefore he was sending his young son to safety in* Eretz Yisrael, *so that some remnant of his family would remain.*

Avrohom was raised in the holy city of Teveria, surrounded by prominent Slonimer Chassidim; truly illustrious luminaries who were privileged to have received their training and guidance from the Kobriner Rebbe and the Yesod HoAvodah. He entered into the yeshivah of Harav Moshe Kliers, Chief Rabbi of Teveria, and grew in Torah and piety. During his lifetime he managed to complete learning the entire Talmud Bavli *and* Yerushalmi *several times.*

He traveled to Europe at the age of 17 to receive instruction from Harav Shmuel, the Slonimer Rebbe. There he absorbed a deep appreciation for loftier planes of avodas Hashem, *qualities that characterized him for the rest of his life.*

More than thirty years later, when the terrible news reached Eretz Yisrael *that the last Slonimer Rebbe had perished in the Holocaust, Rav Avrohom was urged to accept the helm of leadership. He refused adamantly, and Harav Mordechai Chaim [Rav Mottel Slonimer] was selected as the Rebbe. Only upon the passing of Rav Mottel in 5714/1954, did Rav Avrohom acquiesce and accept the position. He served for twenty-seven years as the leader of Slonimer* Chassidus. *During this period, he was successful in raising an entire generation to unparalleled heights in* avodas Hashem, *placing his greatest emphasis on the development of* emunah. *He passed away on 12 Sivan, 5741/1981. Slonimer* Chassidus *continues to thrive under the leadership of his esteemed offspring.*

For many years prior to his assuming the mantle of leadership as the Slonimer Rebbe, Harav Avrohom Weinberg was the dynamic leader of Slonimer Chassidim in Teveria (Tiberias). In partnership with Rav Mottel Slonimer, he was greatly successful in establishing institutions of Torah and chesed throughout the city.

One time, a scalawag in Teveria verbally abused him in a shameful manner. As was his lifelong style, he accepted the insults amiably, without the slightest response. His behavior was in line with the lofty standards set forth by the Sages: "The pasuk states [about] those who are ready to take insults without responding in kind... 'And His loved ones will shine (in Gan Eden) like the sun at the peak of its brilliance.'" (Yoma 23a)

Barely a day had passed and this impertinent individual approached Rav Avrohom, asking for help. The man was in dire financial straits and turned to Rav Avrohom to arrange a loan for him. The man's demeanor was that of a bosom friend, as if nothing untoward had transpired between them the day before. Rav Avrohom welcomed him graciously and with proper respect, perhaps with even more respect than customary, so as to erase any possible ill feeling he might be harboring toward the man. He arranged a sizable loan for him with very favorable conditions.

When Harav Asher Werner, Chief Rabbi of Teveria, learned of this story, he commented, "Actually I am not that surprised that Rav Avrohom worked so diligently to secure a loan for him, despite the fellow's impudence. After all, this trait characterizes Rav Avrohom's superior moral fiber: he is always ready to forgive and forget.

"What does amaze me is the audacity of the man. It must be that Rav Avrohom's crystal character is so well known throughout the city that this individual wasn't a bit self-conscious about the inconsistency of his actions, taking it for granted that he does not even owe Rav Avrohom an apology for his repulsive behavior."

Indeed, how appropriate are *Shlomo HaMelech's* words in *Koheles*: "*Tov shem mishemen tov* — A good name is even more valuable than the finest of oils."

"Hashem, Guard My Tongue From Evil"

Harav Aaron Kotler

*Rosh Yeshivah, Kletzk Yeshivah
and Beth Medrash Govoha*

"Hashem, Guard My Tongue From Evil"

Harav Aaron Kotler zt"l, Rosh Yeshivah of Beth Medrash Govoha in Lakewood, New Jersey was born in Lithuania in 5652/1892. When Aaron was only 10, his father, Harav Shneur Zalman, Rav of Sislowitz, died. Two years later, he lost his mother as well. Despite his personal misfortunes, he immersed himself entirely in Torah study at the yeshivah of Harav Zalman Sender Kahane-Shapiro in Kriniki. Displaying phenomenal intellectual capacity, he progressed to the great Torah seminary in Slobodka where he earned his place of distinction as one of its elite students. The famous Mashgiach of the yeshivah, Harav Nosson Notta Finkel, felt especially close to the lad and guided him toward his future role as a leader of Klal Yisrael.

When Rav Aaron was 20, the famous sage Harav Isser Zalman Meltzer, Rosh Yeshivah of the Yeshivah of Slutzk, chose him as his son-in-law. When the Bolsheviks seized power in 5677/1917, the yeshivah moved to Kletzk, Poland. Shortly thereafter, Rav Isser Zalman immigrated to Eretz Yisrael and the leadership of the yeshivah was passed to Rav Aaron. He became well known as the Kletzker Rosh Yeshivah, a title that followed him for the rest of his life. For the next twenty years, until the onset of World War II, he stood at the helm of the Kletzk Yeshivah, one of the prime Torah centers of Lithuania.

With the outbreak of the war, he escaped to Vilna. In 5701/1941, he arrived in the United States where he immediately thrust himself into rescue work through the Vaad Hatzalah *organization.*

In 5704/1944 he established Beth Medrash Govoha in Lakewood, which eventually grew to become the largest Torah bastion in America. The fire of Torah that burned within his soul ignited thousands of American-born youth. Through his example, they were inspired to discard materialistic values and dedicate themselves totally to advancement in Torah. In addition to his numerous duties at the yeshivah, Rav Aaron was deeply involved in all facets of Jewish education, in America and in Israel, as well as with myriad congregational and charitable organizations and individuals.

He passed away on 2 Kislev, 5723/1962 and was laid to rest next to his father-in- law, Rav Isser Zalman, in Yerushalayim. Leadership of the Lakewood yeshivah was passed on to his only son.

One of the students at Beth Medrash Govoha in Lakewood had the special privilege of serving the *Rosh Yeshivah* his daily cup of coffee during the days he spent in Lakewood, generally twice per week. One day, after placing the coffee on his *rebbe's* desk, the student passed the office and noticed that the cup was untouched.

He slipped in, removed the cold cup of coffee and returned with a piping hot replacement, assuming that the *Rosh*

Yeshivah, Harav Aaron Kotler, had simply forgotten his coffee because he was so engrossed in his studies. Several minutes later, he passed by the office, noticing that again the coffee remained untouched. At this point, the student realized that it was not merely a matter of concentration; there must have been a distinct reason. With proper apologies he approached his *rebbe* for an explanation.

"I'll share my thoughts with you," Rav Aaron remarked. "A certain family with whom I'm friendly is taking an interest in a former student of the yeshivah regarding a marriage prospect. It is very likely that they will call me to inquire about him.

"Praising him with attributes he does not possess is a Torah prohibition on two counts, *midvar sheker tirchak* — 'distance yourself from words of falsehood' — as well as *lo saamod al dam reiacho* — 'do not be oblivious to the spilling of another person's blood,' for if unknown negative traits ultimately lead to discord or divorce, it is directly attributable to the fact that honest information was withheld. On the other hand, I don't feel comfortable divulging my true feelings, since there is always the possibility that, once married, the couple will be happy with one another. My remarks might very well cause the needless disintegration of a *shidduch*.

"It is indeed an awesome responsibility that I'm facing. For this reason I have designated this day as a day of fasting and prayer to *Hashem* that He grant me a kindness and spare me from this call."

This anecdote was related to the late *Rosh Yeshivah* of Manchester, Harav Yehuda Zev Segal, while he was visiting the United States. He was so inspired by Rav Aaron's meticulousness in guarding each word he uttered, that he remarked: "Had I come to America just to hear this beautiful story, it would have sufficed."

Fulfillment Despite Terrible Pain

Harav
Nochum
Partzovitz

Rosh Yeshivah, Mirrer Yeshivah

Fulfillment Despite Terrible Pain

*Harav Nochum Partzovitz zt"l, Rosh Yeshivah of
the Mirrer Yeshivah of Yerushalayim, was born in
5683/1923 in Truky, Lithuania, where his father,
Harav Zvi Arye, was the Rav. Because he had a
prodigious mind, he was sent to Vilna at the tender
age of 10 to study at the famous Rameiles Yeshivah.
After three years, he continued on to Baranovitch,
where he became one of the outstanding students
of Harav Elchonon Wasserman.*

*After four years of intense study, he moved on to
Kamenitz to hear the lectures of its illustrious Rosh
Yeshivah, Harav Boruch Ber Leibowitz. His
outstanding diligence and razor sharp penetration
into the most complex of Talmudic subjects earned
his Rosh Yeshivah's assessment that he would
eventually grow up to become the Rabbi Akiva Eiger
of his generation.*

*In 5699/1939, he arrived in Mir and became
attached to this great Torah institution for the rest of his
life. He joined the yeshivah in its wanderings to Vilna
at the outbreak of World War II and throughout its
sojourn to Shanghai, China. During those six years he
became known as a true Torah giant.*

*After the war, he lived for a short while in America.
In 5709/1949 he immigrated to Eretz Yisrael and*

married the daughter of the Mirrer Rosh Yeshivah,
Harav Chaim Shmulevitz. Shortly after, he began
lecturing in the Mirrer Yeshivah. His sessions were
outstanding in their originality and penetration.

During the last fifteen years of his life he was
afflicted with an incurable disease, which caused him
terrible pain. Despite all obstacles, Rav Nochum
persisted in his superhuman diligence in Torah study
and some of his most profound lectures were
formulated during those trying years. He attracted
large crowds to his lectures, not only from among his
own students, but from throughout Yerushalayim.

By the time Rav Nochum passed away on
18 Cheshvan, 5757/1997, he was recognized
as a respected Torah scholar. He left behind
a generation of marbitzei Torah *who carry on*
his work.

Throughout the fifteen years that Harav Nochum Partzovitz was afflicted with a debilitating disease, he never uttered a single complaint, despite the intense pain. Only once did he share his suffering with one of his students, and even then only for a specific purpose.

The student had come to him to pour out his heart about his own terrible sickness, a condition for which medical science had no cure, which kept him almost constantly in unbearable pain. The whole time Rav Nochum listened attentively, often crying with the man, sharing his anguish. After several minutes, he said:

"You surely know that I too am sick. I will divulge to you something I've refrained from discussing with others. My pain is constant and excruciating, to the degree that I often wonder how I am able to tolerate it. As you can see, each step I take is an agonizing struggle. The challenge is to stand up to it and to realize that a wealth of spiritual strength can be mustered from it.

"Think about it," he said as he turned to his former student with compassion. "Both of us are fortunate to have our Torah study deepened because we are challenged by affliction, an opportunity that most people never live to attain. Shouldn't this in itself be a great source of happiness?"

It was not until much later that the students of the Mirrer Yeshivah gained new insights into the essence of life itself, through the *mesiras nefesh* of Rav Nochum:

One day, a student was engaged in a complex Talmudic discussion with Rav Nochum when he noticed that the *Rav's* eye focused momentarily on a visitor who had just walked through the doorway of the *beis medrash*. He did not attribute great significance to the fleeting diversion. His *rebbe* continued the discussion for a long time, until every facet of the problem had been resolved.

After the student returned to his seat, he watched Rav Nochum rush over to the visitor, hugging and kissing him in an outpouring of emotion. A short time later, he learned that the man was a childhood friend of the *Rosh Yeshivah* who had traveled to Israel with one objective in mind: to persuade Rav Nochum to come to America for medical treatments. After Rav Nochum deliberated the matter carefully, the proposal was rejected.

That day, the entire student body of the yeshivah (more than 1,000 at the time) grasped the deep significance of the verse *ki azah k'mavess ahavah* — "Love is as strong as death." Even the natural human instinct to seek a cure, however remote the possibility for success, did not rival Rav Nochum's love of Torah. It became clear to them that he was attached to the Torah with every strand of his soul — and nothing else mattered.

An Inspiring Precedent

Another aspect of finding spiritual joy through affliction may be gained from the following story concerning the *Alter* of Slobodka, which this author was privileged to hear from a prominent lecturer in *mussar*.

The lecturer related that the *Alter* of Slobodka, Harav Nosson Notta Finkel, commented on the Sages' interpretation of the verse כל הנשמה תהלל י-ה — "the entire soul shall thank *Hashem*"— that the word נשמה (*neshomah*, soul) also reflects the word נשימה, (*neshimah*, breathing). Consequently, על כל נשימה ונשימה חייב להודות, man must thank *Hashem* for every single breath [נשימה]. Additionally, the *Alter* commented, not only does man owe gratitude for each breath, he must thank *Hashem* even if the only thing he possesses is his breath.

Following the lecture, I respectfully questioned the logic of offering gratitude when one possesses nothing but his breath. My question was based on the Sages' comment that the words "very good," used by *Hashem* at the end of Creation, refers to death. (*Bereshis* 1:31 — "And G-d saw all that He had made, and behold it was very good.") This statement assumes that when one reaches the terminal stage of life, when each breath is a chore, *Hashem* in His infinite wisdom determines that the time has come to end life, and the term used for it is "very good." If so, why should a person thank *Hashem* when he has nothing left but spasms of irregular, grueling gasps, the last moments before dying?

"Let me relate a most fascinating anecdote to you," he answered. "When the *Alter* of Slobodka was on his deathbed, he was cared for by one of his most devoted students, one who was privileged to have studied under his guidance in Europe, prior to their migration to *Eretz Yisrael*.

"When the student realized that the end was nearing, he addressed his master and said: 'I beg your forgiveness for my brazenness in asking this question, but I'm certain that you agree that I have been a faithful student for many years. The only reason for my question is my sincere desire to comprehend an observation often stated by you, my teacher and master.'

"'Ask my son, ask,' the *Alter* encouraged him.

"The student began nervously and with apparent hesitation, but finally, he managed to articulate his question. 'As a lifelong disciple, I have heard you comment that כל הנשמה תהלל י-ה means not only that for each נשימה, for each breath, we must thank *Hashem*, but also, that when a person possesses nothing but his breath he must offer gratitude to *Hashem*. Would the *rebbe* kindly elaborate on this comment?'

"'My dear son, listen carefully to what I will now tell you,' the *Alter* said with his last bit of energy. 'A person approaching the very end of life, when he possesses absolutely nothing but a gulp of air, is still a very rich man. He still possesses an immeasurable wealth that no one can remove from him: his ability to unite his thoughts with his Creator, and to observe for another moment the phenomenal *mitzvah* of *ahavas Hashem* — love of G-d, and the *mitzvah* of *yiras Hashem* — fear of G-d. These are the most treasured moments in a person's entire life, to which no monetary value can be affixed. If only I had the physical strength, I would dance and rejoice at this wonderful, once-in-a-lifetime opportunity I now have.'

"That night, the *tzaddik* and sage — the *Alter* of Slobodka — returned his holy *neshomah* to his Creator."

Absolute Faith in the Power of Tehillim

Harav Eliyahu Dushnitzer

Mashgiach, Lomza Yeshivah

Absolute Faith in the Power of Tehillim

Harav Eliyahu Dushnitzer zt"l, Mashgiach of Yeshivas Lomza in Petach Tikvah, was born in 5636/1876 in a town near Lomza. In his youth, he learned in Telshe and Slobodka. He was later educated in Radin, in the company of the illustrious Chofetz Chaim, who became his role model for his entire life. He was a member of the distinguished Kollel Kodoshim *in Radin, which included the world-renowned Rav Elchonon Wasserman.*

With the establishment of the Lomza Yeshivah in Petach Tikvah in 5686/1926, he immigrated to Eretz Yisrael *to assume the position of* Mashgiach Ruchani. *In the twenty-three years that he lived in the Holy Land, till his passing, he was successful in having a major impact on his students and on the yeshivah world at large. Many a young man alienated from Judaism changed his goals and aspirations as a result of his exposure to Rav Eliyahu.*

In addition to his educational activities at the yeshivah, *he was also most active in elevating the spiritual status of the city of Petach Tikvah, especially in the area of Sabbath observance. Many a shopkeeper who had previously kept his store open on Shabbos eventually closed it in deference to Rav Eliyahu, "the* tzaddik *of Petach Tikvah."*

*His diligence in Torah study was extraordinary and
had a great impact on the student body, encouraging
each to reach for the upper limits of his potential. It is
noteworthy that when his life's partner of scores of
years passed away, he made sure that her funeral
procession would be scheduled for the midday
break at the yeshivah, so as to minimize the* bitul
Torah *of the students.*

Reb Eliyahu passed away on 22 Av, 5709/1949.

Rav Eliyahu Dushnitzer had a son who moved from *Eretz
Yisrael* to America. Wishing to provide his father with some
form of income, he gave him an orange grove in Ramat
Hasharon. Shortly thereafter, however, the citrus industry went
into an economic crisis and many growers were forced into
bankruptcy. Not only did the grove not produce income, it
incurred large deficits.

Rav Eliyahu was utterly distressed, constantly worrying that
if his time should come to depart from this world, he will have
left over debts. This prospect troubled him greatly, since the
Sages term a deadbeat debtor a *rasha*, a wicked man.

What then could be the solution to his grave problem? To
Rav Eliyahu, the answer was simple enough: Turn to Father
and ask him to resolve his predicament. And that's exactly
what he did. He pleaded to *Hashem*, our Father in heaven. In
addition, whoever came in contact with him was asked to pray
on his behalf.

One of his students, upon leaving his studies at the *kollel*,
entered the field of real estate. Aware of Rav Eliyahu's
problem, the student found the ideal buyer for the grove, a
well-to-do American who had expressed great interest in

buying some agricultural property in *Eretz Yisrael*. He arranged a meeting between the prospective buyer and Rav Eliyahu, and all three took a bus from Petach Tikvah to Ramat Hasharon to inspect the orchard.

No sooner had they started the trip than Rav Eliyahu turned to the American with a solemn expression and said, "I wish to perform the great *mitzvah* of ולא תונו איש את אמיתו, not to deceive a customer. I therefore want to inform you of the orchard's various shortcomings. Several trees have become insect infested. Others dried up or have rotted away. Also, in some places, the soil has developed ditches and pits due to neglect. In short, from an economic standpoint, the grove at present is truly problematic."

Rav Eliyahu then proceeded to coach the man in what he understood to be good business sense. "If your objective is to buy the property for investment purposes and return overseas, I must share with you what our Sages have advised: 'If one wishes to lose his money he should hire workers and not be with them.' In short, absentee management is a prescription for financial disaster. So if your plan is to return to America and to manage it from afar, it is not a wise investment."

The prospective buyer listened attentively but did not seem overly concerned, continuing to show interest in the orchard. When they finally arrived at the site, Rav Eliyahu again turned to the man and said: "Our Sages have said that there is no comparison between actually seeing something to having merely heard about it. Now that we are here, I wish to take you on a guided tour and point out every decayed tree, all of the insect-infested trees, as well as the pits and ditches."

Surprisingly, despite having seen all the negative aspects of the grove, the prospective buyer still did not seem to be dissuaded from the sale. During the conversation, the man took some pills and a small container of water out of his pocket and gulped down the pills. He explained that he suffered from a heart problem and must take medication regularly.

The man barely had a chance to conclude his sentence when Rav Eliyahu declared in no uncertain terms that he was retracting his offer. He was adamant that under no circumstances was he ready to sell the property to him. The man was shocked, not comprehending the sudden change of heart on the part of Rav Eliyahu.

"Kindly explain this to me," he asked Rav Eliyahu in a state of disbelief. "I heard everything you had to say, including all the drawbacks of the property, and yet I am interested. Why then the sudden retraction?"

"I am truly sorry for all the bother and inconvenience I caused you in traveling here in vain," Rav Eliyahu said apologetically. "However, I just realized that the Torah does not allow me to proceed with the sale. Let me explain. As soon as I became aware that you have a heart problem, I realized that you are not fit for the laborious, backbreaking work of agriculture. You will therefore have to employ farmhands to assist you, and your primary function will be management. The fact is that the grove is much too small to support a full-time manager, and the result will be absentee management. This I cannot allow under any circumstances, as our Sages have ruled that it is a sure way to lose one's money."

As expected, the deal did not go through. The American returned to the United States and Rav Eliyahu returned to continued losses from his orange grove.

Several days passed and Rav Eliyahu happened to meet one of his favorite former students, the venerable *Maggid* of Yerushalayim, Harav Sholom Shwadron.

"I have a special request for you, dear Reb Sholom," he said. "Were you not someone very close to me, I would feel uncomfortable asking it of you. You're surely aware of all the aggravation I've been having from my orange grove in Ramat Hasharon, and the great deficits it is incurring. May I ask that when you return to Yerushalayim you visit a certain friend of yours who studied alongside you at the yeshivah in Petach Tikvah?

"This friend has established a Talmud Torah in Yerushalayim. Some time ago I met him and poured out my heart to him in regard to this grove. I asked him to recite several chapters of *Tehillim* in my behalf with the schoolchildren every day after their studies."

Reb Sholom noticed that at this point his *rebbe* began speaking haltingly, not ready to express his true feelings. Seemingly, Rav Eliyahu wished to say something about the founder of the Talmud Torah, but could not find the appropriate words, as he did not want to infer even the faintest expression of disappointment.

At last, Rav Eliyahu did find the correct words. "You know, Reb Sholom, your friend is such a busy person — carrying the responsibility for both the educational and budgetary needs of his Talmud Torah — as well as his myriad *chesed* activities. It is no surprise that he overlooked my request regarding reciting *Tehillim* with the children. Please, Rav Sholom, when you arrive in Yerushalayim, kindly approach him and encourage him on my behalf."

"I beg the *rebbe's* forgiveness, Rav Sholom said, "but how are you so sure that my friend actually forgot about the *Tehillim*?"

"That's obvious," Rav Eliyahu replied with absolute conviction. "The fact is that thus far I have been unsuccessful in finding the proper buyer for the property. Unquestionably, the only factor missing is the sincere prayers of the *tinokos shel beis rabban*, the precious Talmud Torah children."

Immediately upon arriving in Yerushalayim, Rav Sholom rushed to the Talmud Torah and met his friend just as he was hurrying from the school. Rav Sholom related his encounter with their *rebbe* and the conversation that ensued. His friend apologetically admitted that he did indeed forget about Rav Eliyahu and his orange grove and had not implemented the request for *Tehillim*. Although he was late for an appointment, he immediately turned back, gathered the children and recited several chapters of *Tehillim* with them.

In less than a week, Rav Eliyahu successfully sold the property to a skilled farmer who found all the orange grove's problems to be minor and easily correctable. He paid full market price for it, enabling Rav Eliyahu to repay all his outstanding obligations. This good fortune did not surprise Rav Eliyahu at all. He had never doubted the power of *Tehillim* from the mouths of the holy children of Yerushalayim.

Upholding the Sanctity of Shabbos

Harav Soliman Mutzapi

author of Ayin HaRekach

Upholding the Sanctity of Shabbos

Harav Soliman Mutzapi zt"l was born in Baghdad in 5660/1900. Baghdad kehillah archives record that members of the Mutzapi family have been either rabbinic or communal leaders for seventeen generations. His paternal grandfather was Harav Yechezkel, Rosh Yeshivah of the Baghdad Yeshivah.

While still a small child, Soliman attended the weekly sermons of Harav Yosef Chaim, the Ben Ish Chai, one of the greatest Sephardic scholars in recent times. The love and fear of Hashem that he absorbed in those primary years served him well for the rest of his life.

As a teenager, Soliman studied under the direction of Harav Yehudah Patya and at age 17 he was ordained by Harav Abdallah Somech. At 25 he began writing his interpretations and insights on Kabbalah, covering most of the classic works on the subject. Eventually he published them in what became known as a masterpiece: Yayin HaRekach. In those years, his learning partner was Harav Nissim Kaduri Chazan, one of Iraq's greatest Torah authorities. Although he easily could have taken a leadership position, he chose to fulfill the Sages' suggestion to "love work and shun pompousness and rank," supporting himself for many years as general

*manager of the business empire of the distinguished
entrepreneur, Mr. Menachem Daniel.*

*In 5694/1934 Horah Mutzapi immigrated to
Eretz Yisrael and joined the beis medrash of the
eminent kabbalist, Harav Chaim Shaul HaKohen
Dwik. He also delved into the insights of the
hallowed Siddur Rashash, under the tutelage of
Harav Yaakov Munsah.*

*He gained fame in Yerushalayim as a sage,
proficient in both Talmudic and kabbalistic studies
and as an exceptionally holy man, detached from all
worldly pleasures. Throughout his life he abstained
from all prepared food, eating only what his wife
prepared at home, and even that, to a bare minimum.*

*His humility and rigorous pursuit of mitzvos
were legendary. His prayers and tikkunim [literally,
mending; in essence, mending the spiritual status of
oneself or others, in a structured fashion] were
remarkable, and many a wayward individual
repented and returned to the fold through his efforts.
His influence on his generation was profound,
especially on the Iraqi Jewish community.*

*He passed away on 17 Teves, 5735/1975 and was
eulogized by the greatest Sephardic and Ashkenazic
Torah sages, all of whom emphasized his outstanding
erudition and lofty tzidkus.*

I n his desire to earn a livelihood from his own labors, and not
from the support of others, Harav Soliman Mutzapi worked for
a while as general manager of the diverse enterprises of
Menachem Daniel, the Iraqi-Jewish magnate. Although engaged

in business full time, Rav Soliman dedicated a minimum of eight hours per day to Torah study.

During his business career, he had many occasions to sanctify *Hashem's* Name in a profound way; to fully execute the *Shulchan Aruch's* guidelines of בכל דרכיך דעהו, "In all your ways know Him." Rav Soliman gracefully exemplified the sanctity of *Klal Yisrael* and its uniqueness as a Torah nation. The following story is but one example of his dedication to this ideal.

A clerk in the employ of the Iraqi Treasury Department arrived one Shabbos afternoon at the residence of Mr. Daniel. He was escorted by the Counsel General of Great Britain and accompanied by a delegation of top industry executives who had just arrived from London. His visit entailed a major international business transaction. Due to its urgency, a clerk was sent to fetch Rav Soliman, for as general manager he was more knowledgeable in the matter than anyone else.

The clerk was directed to a local *beis medrash* where Rav Soliman was learning at the time under the guidance of his *rebbe*, Harav Yehuda Patya. When he arrived, they were in deep concentration, immersed in the holy *sefer Eitz Chaim*, authored by Rav Chaim Vital (the primary disciple of the Ari HaKadosh).

When told of the purpose of the clerk's visit, Rav Soliman realized that he had two options. One course would be to send a message excusing himself from the meeting, due to the sanctity of Shabbos. However, Rav Soliman chose an approach that was more circuitous, but one that would demonstrate the significance of Shabbos and the central role it plays in the life of a Jew.

Rav Soliman strode with the messenger through the wide boulevards of Baghdad's central business district, dressed in his traditional Oriental rabbinic attire — a white silk kaftan, with a shining golden turban. When they reached Mr. Daniel's expansive corporate headquarters, they found the entire delegation was seated around a conference table, waiting impatiently for the arrival of the general manager. Upon arrival, the *Rav* introduced himself and welcomed each one with his well-known enthusiastic handshake. He apologized for momentarily leaving the room, and returned immediately from his private office with a clock in his hand.

"My dear distinguished friends, it is now 4:45 p.m. In two and three-quarter hours, the sun will set and the stars will illuminate the skies, signaling the departure of Jewry's queen, the holy Sabbath. I ask your indulgence until that time, in deference to this holy day that symbolizes the bond between the Creator and His people."

The assembled were obviously disappointed at the sudden postponement of their plans, especially in light of their overbooked schedule. Not having other alternatives, they reluctantly acquiesced.

Rav Soliman returned to his *rebbe* in the *beis medrash* and began to dance, so great was his joy at having demonstrated reverence for the holy Sabbath.

When Shabbos was over, Rav Soliman rushed back to the office and a pleasant surprise awaited him. Upon entering, the entire group gave him a standing ovation. The Consul General of Great Britain was the spokesman for the entire group in his articulation of their feelings: "Master Mutzapi, now, more than ever, we are convinced of your righteousness and honesty; that despite the great pressures you were facing, you stood up for your religious convictions with dignity. It is indeed an honor for us to negotiate major transactions with a gentleman of your caliber."

Throughout his life, Rav Soliman reminisced about this incident and commented: "Never before did I feel such elation and identification with the *kedushas haShabbos* as on that Shabbos. Some of the greatest government officials and business tycoons, each anxious to proceed with a major international deal, all had to put their plans aside in deference to the majestic queen — *Shabbos HaMalkah.*"

The Imprisoned Cry

Harav Eliezer Zusia Portugal

Skulener Rebbe

The Imprisoned Cry

*Harav Eliezer Zusia Portugal zt"l, the Skulener Rebbe,
was born in 5658/1898 in the town Skulen on the
Romanian-Russian border. His father, Harav Yisrael
Avraham, served as the Rav of the town, and was a
disciple of Harav Yeshaya Shur, Rav of Yassi, a pupil of
Harav Mordechai of Kremnitz. Harav Mordechai was
the son of Reb Mechele Zlotchiver, one of the elite
adherents of the Baal Shem Tov.*

*When his father passed away, the town's elders,
with the encouragement of the Romanian Torah
sages, chose Rav Eliezer Zusia to take on the
position of Rav, though he was only 17 years old. As
a result of his phenomenal success in Skulen, he
was invited to the city of Chernowitz. He was most
successful there in strengthening Yiddishkeit in many
areas, but primarily in establishing an exemplary
yeshivah school system. With his outstanding
educational capabilities, he created a revolution
among the youth, returning many to the fold.*

*Following World War II, after the fall of
Chernowitz to the Communist forces, he relocated
to Bucharest, Romania's capital. Recognizing the
need of the hour, he began an intensive campaign
on behalf of Holocaust orphans. Through the years
he personally raised hundreds of orphans in his*

own home; and at the first opportunity he smuggled them out of the country, to Israel or to the West.

In 5706/1946 the Communists occupied Romania. They warned the Skulener Rebbe on numerous occasions that they viewed his activities most unfavorably. A devoted father to his orphaned charges, he disregarded Communist threats and, together with his noble Rebbetzin, dedicated himself totally to the task of raising their "children." Through the years, the Rebbe and his only son were imprisoned on numerous occasions and were systematically tortured for not revealing the identity of Jews who were suspected of engaging in economic offenses.

Through international intervention on his behalf, he was permitted to leave Romania. Upon arrival in America, the Rebbe began an intensive campaign to rescue all the Jews languishing in Romanian prisons. Even in situations where there seemed to be no hope, he did not despair and, more often than not, his efforts were crowned with success. In tandem with his activities on behalf of their physical security, the Rebbe worked relentlessly for their spiritual well-being, establishing the internationally famous organization Chesed L'Avraham toward that objective.

He passed away on erev Rosh Chodesh Elul, 5742/1982. Leadership of the Skulener community and of Chesed L'Avraham are continued by his only son.

I n 5716/1956 a revolution broke out against the Communist establishment in Hungary. The pro-democratic forces fought valiantly against the dictatorial regime, but to no avail. Russia sent in a large division of its armed forces with modern tanks and military hardware and quashed the rebellion with brute force.

The Hungarian revolution had a direct impact on its neighboring countries, specifically, Romania. Although Communism had arrived there many years before, the Romanian government tightened its grip on its population as never before, lest the spirit of democracy from Hungary spill over into their country. The new reign of terror saw scores of rabbis, *shochtim* and other Jewish religious functionaries jailed. Many ordinary Jewish citizens were also arrested and tortured to obtain their "confessions" of economic crimes against the state. Many were condemned to long prison sentences.

In those bitter days, the rescue work of Harav Eliezer Zusia Portugal became so much more difficult. Military censorship affected all overseas communications; hence, it was impossible to arouse world opinion against governmental oppression. Most solicitations for funds to be used for *pidyon shvuyim* — prisoner release — came to a grinding halt.

Ironically, the Romanian government tried hard to give the impression of being a compassionate regime, especially in regard to its Jewish population. From time to time the government brought important personalities from abroad to demonstrate to them the high quality of life enjoyed by its Jewish citizens. As expected, these visitors — traveling at government expense and escorted throughout their tour by official "guides" — saw nothing amiss. All meetings between them and Romanian Jews took place in the presence of governmental informers. Not surprisingly, the Jews they met spoke gloriously of the "wonderful, democratic government of Romania," simply out of fear of imprisonment.

One of the distinguished personalities officially brought to visit the Jewish population was the Chief Rabbi of Sweden,

Rabbi Dr. Yaakov Dovid (Kurt) Wilhelm, who had been educated in world-class universities. He associated with nobility and the aristocracy worldwide and, corresponding to his international stature, his influence was enormous.

The first week Rabbi Wilhelm spent as an official guest of the government, and the following week, as the guest of the Jewish community of Bucharest. The Central Jewish Organization of Bucharest arranged a grand *Melaveh Malkah* in his honor, inviting all rabbis and Jewish functionaries. They knew well that the visit was just a massive sham, but they all attended, as there was no alternative; boycotting the affair could result in a prison sentence.

Immediately after Shabbos, all the invited guests hurried to the *Melaveh Malkah* — that is, all except for the Skulener Rebbe, who continued his normal custom of extolling "the Sabbath Queen" for two hours beyond the conventional time.

The Rebbe finally arrived, and the entire assemblage rose in his honor. He was led to take his place at the dais next to Rabbi Rosen, Chief Rabbi of Romania. The Swedish guest openly displayed his surprise at the respect accorded to this gaunt, diminutive Chassidic rabbi sporting an ancient *shtreimel* on his head. Rabbi Rosen explained to Rabbi Wilhelm that Romanian Jewry considered the man an unequivocal *tzaddik* and sage.

Speaker after speaker highlighted the living paradise of Romania, declaring that life could not be better for any Jew anywhere in the world. At the culmination of the speeches, Rabbi Rosen called on the Skulener Rebbe to lead the audience in singing one of his melodies, for he was reputed to be a master composer of Chassidic music. The Rebbe began singing his heartrending composition תבא לפניך אנקת אסיר — "Let the groan of the prisoner come before You," a song that symbolizes the pain of prison inmates who cry in anguish and pray for deliverance. The Rebbe sang the *nigun* with an outpouring of passion, crying incessantly; bemoaning the afflicted status of his incarcerated brethren.

Our Sages have assured, "Words flowing from the heart will surely penetrate another's heart." Rabbi Wilhelm was overcome with emotion from this truly moving song, fully comprehending the covert message the Rebbe had intended to convey about the depressing state of Romanian Jewry. He knew beyond a doubt that they were collectively imprisoned and cry out to *Hashem* for freedom. Above all, the Rebbe's personality touched a chord in his heart.

During the next few days, Rabbi Wilhelm had the opportunity to visit the Rebbe several times and his impact on his Swedish guest was indeed extraordinary. Upon leaving the country, Rabbi Wilhelm told the Rebbe that finally, after years of searching, he had found a true guide. In a follow-up letter to Rabbi Rosen he wrote about the Skulener Rebbe, stating: "My heart is tied to his heart."

Years passed and the situation in Romania deteriorated to the point that, in 5719/1959, the Rebbe and his son were arrested and brutally tortured. Appeals from the entire free world poured in for their release, but to no avail. The tyrannical Romanian government knew no bounds, and the lives of the Rebbe and his son were in imminent danger.

That year, the Satmar Rebbe, Harav Yoel Teitelbaum, visited London. Among the people he met was Mr. Aaron (Harry) Goodman, president of Zeirei Agudath Yisrael of Great Britain, a fiery activist for *Chareidi* Judaism. The Satmar Rebbe implored him to use his extensive connections for the release of the Skulener Rebbe and his son, adding, that financial considerations should in no way play a role. He would assume all expenses.

Mr. Goodman explained that his organization had invested all possible resources on behalf of the Rebbe, with no success, and that cost considerations had never entered the picture. He added that the only person who might have an influence on the Romanian government was Dag Hammarskjold, secretary-general of the United Nations, but nobody in the British

Agudah had access to him. "We know, however, that Mr. Hammarskjold does have a close Jewish friend, a childhood chum who grew up with him from kindergarten through university," Mr. Goodman remarked. "His name is Kurt Wilhelm and he serves as Chief Rabbi of Sweden. But I doubt that he would help us."

The Satmar Rebbe listened attentively to Mr. Goodman's presentation, but insisted that regardless of the slim chances of success, all attempts should be made to contact the Swedish rabbi.

Mr. Goodman immediately telephoned Rabbi Wilhelm's home in Stockholm. He was told that the Rabbi was out of the country. In fact, he was in England, staying at a hotel in London. Hearing this, Mr. Goodman immediately realized that the hand of *Hashem* was at work. He contacted the hotel, and fortuitously, he was immediately connected with the rabbi. They set up a meeting for that very day.

At their meeting, Mr. Goodman explained that he came to discuss a most sensitive subject, the imprisonment of a great rabbi named Portugal who, together with his only son, was being tortured in a Romanian dungeon on trumped-up charges. He had barely finished the sentence, when Dr. Wilhelm burst out in a wail, repeating incessantly: "I can't believe what I'm hearing! This is my *rebbe*, a truly holy man, whose very existence is a sanctification of G-d's Name!"

He immediately called the Romanian Foreign Ministry, requesting a visa. When questioned as to the purpose of his visit, he replied innocently that his objective was to meet certain government officials regarding the Portugal case. His request was arrogantly denied. "You're surely aware that the Portugals were arrested on serious criminal charges. Unlike the court systems in the West, the Romanian judicial system is independent of external influences. We judge cases solely on merit and not through influence peddling."

When the Swedish Chief Rabbi realized that he would not succeed with a direct approach, he devised a circuitous strategy.

He notified his family that he would not be returning from London right away, flying instead to New York to take care of some critically important matters. Upon his arrival in New York, he immediately rushed to the home of his friend, Dag Hammarskjold. The rabbi outlined the noble character of the Skulener Rebbe and described him as one the world's greatest humanitarians who had selflessly devoted his efforts to the care of countless war orphans. He and his wife had raised many of them in their own home.

"I would venture to say that you were Providentially placed in this high position as secretary-general of the United Nations for this task, as Mordechai says in the Book of Esther: 'And who knows whether it was just for such a time as this that you attained the royal position.'"

Mr. Hammarskjold was visibly moved. He immediately sent a forceful memorandum to the Romanian government appealing for the release of Rabbi Portugal and his son. When a satisfactory reply was not forthcoming, he flew to Bucharest to intervene personally. At the same time, the president of the United States, Dwight D. Eisenhower, urged to take action by leaders of the Jewish community, pressed for the release of the rabbi and his son. To satisfy immigration law requirements, K'hal Adas Yereim [the "*Viener Shul*"] sent an affidavit requesting Rabbi Portugal to assume the prestigious position of spiritual leader of their congregation, one of the largest in Brooklyn, New York.

Baruch Hashem, the prayers of *Klal Yisrael* were answered, as the Psalmist states in *Tehillim* (142:8):

"הוציאה ממסגר נפשי להודות את שמך בי יכתרו צדיקים כי תגמל עלי." —
"Release my soul from confinement to acknowledge Your Name; the righteous will crown themselves with me, when You bestow kindness upon me."

The Rebbe, his son and their families were allowed to leave the country via Antwerp for their final destination, the United States.

Indeed, how appropriate are the words of the Skulener Rebbe in his *sefer, Noam Eliezer,* on the above verse, תבא לפניך

אנקת אסיר — "Let the groan of the prisoner come before You." There, he quotes Harav Sholom Rokeach, the first Belzer Rebbe, who interprets the word אסיר, prisoner, as referring not only to the person [who is jailed], but also to the imprisoned groan: for in some situations, even the cry of anguish, the groan of the prisoner must be suppressed, as he must feign happiness.

Commenting on that interpretation, the Skulener Rebbe writes that after suffering through the Holocaust, many of the survivors wound up living under Communist regimes where they were arrested and sentenced to stiff prison sentences. Even those not arrested were considered incarcerated, forced to live under oppression and the denial of human and religious rights. In those countries, the mere groan — expressing unhappiness with the regime — was cause enough for imprisonment.

Thus, *Dovid HaMelech* writes in *Tehillim:* "תבא לפניך אנקת אסיר" — "Let the groan of the prisoner come before You," beseeching that *Hashem* allow, at a minimum, that the imprisoned groan should be released, enabling the sufferers to vent their sorrow.

A Glimpse of
Extraordinary Humility

Harav
Yaakov
Yisrael
Kanievsky

The Steipler Gaon

A Glimpse of Extraordinary Humility

*Harav Yaakov Yisrael Kanievsky zt"l, was born in 5659/1899 in the town of Horn**steipel**: throughout his life he was referred to as "the Steipler," a shortened version of the name of his birthplace. His father, Harav Chaim Peretz, was a fervent follower of Harav Mordechai Dov Hornsteipler (son-in-law of the Divrei Chaim) and named him after his rebbe's grandfather, Harav Yaakov Yisrael of Cherkas.*

The boy was sent to Hummel, Russia, at a young age to study Torah under the guidance of the "Alter [Elder] of Navarodok." There, he dedicated himself with a singular intensity to toiling in Torah and refined his conduct to a highly pious level, characteristics that remained with him throughout his life.

Days of anguish ensued for the yeshivah following the Bolshevik Revolution in 5677/1917. Harassment and persecution were the order of the day; this, in addition to the normal wartime deprivations of food and clothing. The Alter's students exhibited outstanding self-sacrifice, maintaining their Yiddishkeit under unmanageable conditions. Their steadfastness infuriated the Bolsheviks, and the yeshivah boys — including Yaakov Yisrael — were indiscriminately conscripted into the Soviet army. There, the Steipler's greatness surfaced even more, for despite intolerance and open hostility, he did not waver in his absolute commitment to avodas Hashem and the exacting performance of mitzvos.

Upon his discharge from the army, he rededicated himself to spreading Torah in accordance with the specific style of his revered rebbe. He traveled from town to town and established elementary and advanced yeshivos throughout Russia. When it became apparent that an immediate threat to his life was looming due to these activities, he escaped to Bialystok, Poland, the base of Navarodok operations outside of Russia, headed by the Alter's son-in-law, Harav Avrohom Yoffen.

In 5685/1925 he published his first sefer, Shaarei T'vunah, on complex Talmudic issues. When the Chazon Ish came upon the sefer, he was so impressed that he proposed a match between his sister and the author.

After the wedding, the Steipler served as Rosh Yeshivah of the Navarodok yeshivos in Semiatitz and Pinsk. On the advice of the Chazon Ish, he and his family immigrated to Eretz Yisrael in 5694/1934. Upon arrival, he served for a while as Rosh Yeshivah of the Navarodok yeshivah in Bnei Brak.

Eventually, he was able to dedicate himself totally to the study of Torah and to writing Kehillas Yaakov, a multi-volume work that has become a classic. It has been printed and reprinted in several editions and today is regarded as a standard text throughout the yeshivah world.

Following the passing of the Chazon Ish in 5714/1954, the Steipler became his unofficial successor. His fame as a holy sage (of the caliber of previous generations) spread throughout the world. All roads led to his humble home in Bnei Brak from *where a beacon of light illuminated Jewish life in Israel and across the globe.*

The Steipler returned his soul to his Creator on 23 Av, 5745/1985. It is estimated that approximately 200,000 people came to pay their last respects, the largest funeral in the history of Bnei Brak. He left behind an outstanding generation, including gedolei hador.

Our Sages in *Pirkei Avos* state that a prime characteristic of a Torah personage is that "his mantle is humility." Throughout the generations, Torah sages have excelled in their modesty and humility. Generally, the more Torah they mastered, the greater their simplicity and humbleness.

The following are excerpts from a letter written by Harav Yaakov Yisrael Kanievsky (known as "the Steipler") to his friend Harav Chaim Kreiswirth, Chief Rabbi of Antwerp. In the letter, the Steipler apologizes for not accepting Harav Kreiswirth's invitation to attend the wedding of one of his children in Belgium. His reason? Concern about a possible *chilul Hashem*.

The reader might be surprised. What possible *chilul Hashem* can ensue from a gathering of such Torah sages in a joyful setting? From an objective perspective, it would seem that the opposite is true — the mere appearance of a sage like the Steipler would surely enhance the standing of *Yiddishkeit*, with its resulting *kiddush Hashem*.

The candid letter speaks volumes about his genuine, extraordinary humility. He lists an array of his shortcomings and states his fear that upon coming to Antwerp his failings will surface. People will be disappointed, wondering, is this really the profile of a *godol b'Yisrael*? The result would be a massive *chilul Hashem*.

He writes:

My preliminary comprehension [of any subject matter] is very weak, not comparable even to that of an average talmid chacham. *Also, my [intellectual] grasp is very problematical. This is the honest truth, without the slightest bit of exaggeration. My memory is feeble, especially now in old age. It has diminished to the extent that, to my great dismay, even subjects considered simple by every* talmid chacham *confuse me. I am not exaggerating, writing about things the way they really are.*

The Steipler continues, stating that even in his hometown of Bnei Brak, those who frequently visit him are aware of his very limited Torah knowledge.

Great Torah scholars often come to me to discuss Torah subjects, thinking that I am a gaon, *but I know as a fact that they leave the house very disappointed, realizing that I do not possess any knowledge beyond theirs.*

As if this were not enough, he even goes a step further, saying:

Those who come to find a Torah sage soon discover that I am literally like an ignoramus in matters of Jewish law. This is also not an exaggeration, rather, an honest assessment.

He then goes on to another topic, the subject of *tzidkus* — piety.

Also, those who come to me wanting to see in me a tzaddik *are generally very disappointed, since they soon discover that, in truth, I am a simple person. In addition, lately my diligence in Torah has slackened greatly, due to aging — and even in earlier times it wasn't satisfactory.*

Reading these excerpts, one becomes absolutely befuddled. Consider this. A man who is known not to have wasted a moment's time from his earliest childhood, within a framework of phenomenal *tzidkus*; one whose piety intensified as the years progressed; a person who toiled in Torah for thirty-six uninterrupted hours [except for necessities] at a time, throughout his life — that person considers himself a simpleton, without any qualities higher than the average person!

The focus of the letter then shifts to the Steipler's reluctance to visit Antwerp:

All these things [the gap between his reputation as a *gaon* and *tzaddik* and his own humble perception of himself] *cause me intense pain and heartache. It's not that my pride is on the line; honestly, I praise* Hashem *that the craving for honor is almost not a factor at all. It's the* chilul Hashem, *G-d forbid. I'm concerned that people will feel, 'If this is a representation of a famous Torah sage, what about all other* talmidei chachomim?' [Are they all so much less than what they're portrayed to be?] *Should people start having these doubts, it would result in a massive deterioration of their entire* yiras Shomayim, *G-d forbid.*

Undoubtedly, upon my arrival in Antwerp, large crowds will come to see the 'celebrity' and they will end up disappointed, finding me to be neither a tzaddik *nor a* gaon. Hashem *knows how much heartache and pain this causes me."*

The Steipler concludes that the reason he went out of his way to share his innermost feelings was so that *his eminence* [Harav Kreiswirth] *should not harbor resentment or annoyance at a lowly pauper like me.*

From the Steipler's point of view, there could have been justified annoyance and resentment on the part of Harav Kreiswirth at the fact that despite his advanced age and frail health the Steipler did not travel thousands of kilometers to attend the wedding of a friend who is neither related nor linked by marriage. And in order to mitigate these "justified feelings," he was forced to go out of his way and divulge the real reason — fear of *chilul Hashem* — hoping that his Belgian friend would understand and forgive.

How apt is the Sages' adage "One who seeks greatness, greatness escapes him; while one who escapes it, greatness follows him."

Although the Steipler's letter speaks for itself of his phenomenal level of humility, let us note several key words in the letter that shed an additional dimension on the subject: "It's not that my pride is at stake; honestly, I thank *Hashem* that the *craving for honor is almost not a factor at all.*"

Reflect for a moment on how many people in the entire world can honestly state about themselves that they are immune to the desire for honor and admiration? The great *tzaddik*, Harav Yitzchak Blazer (Rav Itzele Peterburger), writes in his *sefer, Ohr Yisrael*, about his great *rebbe*, Harav Yisrael Salanter. Wishing to highlight his *rebbe's* out-of-the-ordinary levels of *tzidkus*, he says: "The desires for honor and for money, which are like a net engulfing the entire human race, did not occupy any role whatsoever in his life."

The very fact that the Steipler writes that, "the craving for honor is almost not a factor at all," seems to indicate a total lack of consciousness concerning status and honor. For, were he not on this high level, he could never have felt comfortable ascribing to himself such towering qualities, which only the greatest of the great achieve. The obvious conclusion to be drawn is that he was so removed from the very concepts of honor and dishonor that he was not even cognizant of the fact that the subject is a sensitive issue, and that he inadvertently placed himself into the category of the likes of Rav Yisrael Salanter.

An Inspiring Precedent

The Chasam Sofer made an amazing point in one of his letters regarding humility. He states:

No one among us comprehends to what heights Moshe Rabbeinu's *humility reached, as the Torah itself confers upon him this quality. Nevertheless, viewing and contemplating our* rebbe, *Harav Akiva Eiger, we could at least see some semblance of what humility is in a great measure, and thus have some degree of comprehension of the levels of humility of* Moshe Rabbeinu.

In other words, despite the fact that we have absolute faith in the Torah, which states clearly, "And the man Moshe was exceedingly humble, more than any other person on the face of the earth," reading this verse is not comparable to observing a living person who symbolizes the trait of humility at a high level. When we have the opportunity to view an exceptional living *tzaddik*, we can advance our comprehension of what *Moshe Rabbeinu's* humility could have been.

Perhaps we may expand this concept and likewise infer that having seen the exceptional humility of the Steipler, we can gain some appreciation of what Rabbi Akiva Eiger's humility could have been.

Passages from Rav Akiva Eiger's letters bear out the Chasam Sofer's appraisal. The similarity in style and content of those letters to those of the Steipler is truly remarkable. In various letters, Rabbi Akiva Eiger writes:

...I am very surprised at your honor for coming to knock on the door [turning to him with complex Talmudic queries] of a lowly pauper like me.

...I am a boor without the intelligence of a man, and should have hid in a corner and like a dumb person, not opening my mouth, especially in such a complex matter.

...It is obvious that the matter is simple and easy to understand, but only I, in my paucity [of intellect], am blinded [in comprehension] due to my numerous sins.

...The problem is mine, due to the limitations of comprehension. Believe me, I spent about half an hour to figure out its meaning, but could not decipher it, and I was greatly pained over it; seemingly due to numerous pressures, my mind seems to have become dulled.

The Tzaddik's Deep Insight

Harav
Yochanan
Perlow

Stolin-Karliner Rebbe

The Tzaddik's Deep Insight

Harav Yochanan Perlow zt"l, the Stolin-Karliner Rebbe, was born in 5660/1900. In 5681/1921 he became engaged to the daughter of the Rebbe of Alek. Shortly afterward, his father, Harav Yisroel, passed away in Frankfurt, Germany, during his stay there for medical reasons. On the invitation of Stoliner/Karliner Chassidim residing in Lutzk, he relocated from Stolin to Lutzk and remained there until the outbreak of the war. In 5701/1941, with the Nazi occupation of the city, he escaped at the last moment to the forests and dwelled there among the partisans. He eventually found his way to central Russia, where he lived till the war's end.

Harav Yochanan lost his entire family in the Holocaust, except for one little daughter who survived. Upon arrival at the Displaced Persons camp in Feldafing, Germany, he decided not to divulge his identity so as to better share the lot of his bereaved brethren. It seems, however, that Providence had other plans for him. The secretary general of the American Agudath Israel, the indefatigable activist Reb Elimelech [Mike] Tress, visited the camp on behalf of Agudath Israel. While there, he heard the gabbai call an individual by the name of Yochanan ben Yisroel up to the Torah. He immediately figured out the true identity of this humble Jew, and after the service he addressed him, "Shalom aleichem, *Stoliner Rebbe.*"

In 5706/1946 the Rebbe arrived in Eretz Yisrael and settled in Haifa. From there, his influence spread and he invigorated the Stoliner community, which thirsted for his every word. The Rebbe's American followers invited him to come for a visit. In 5708/1948 he visited the United States and found that Jews there were also in dire need of his leadership. He remained in Williamsburg, Brooklyn at the urging of his American Chassidim. Six years later, despite his declining health, the Rebbe undertook the arduous trip to Eretz Yisrael. Indeed, he was successful in strengthening the spiritual level of his devoted flock there, however, he was forced to cut the visit short and return to America for medical treatments.

On 21 Kislev 5716/1955 he was torn from Klal Yisrael, at the age of 56. He was interred temporarily in America and after a year was re-interred in Teveria, alongside the tomb of Rav Mendele Vitebsker. His grandson continues to lead the Stoliner community in the paths of his ancestors.

student learning in the Stoliner Yeshivah informed his Rebbe, Harav Yochanan Perlow, the joyful news that he recently became engaged to a fine young lady. The Rebbe shared the boy's happiness and wished him great success and a blissful marriage. In the course of the conversation, he encouraged the young man to keep up his regular study schedule with diligence and not be sidetracked with wedding preparations during regular sessions. "Make it a matter of principle to conduct all wedding-related matters during off-hours only," he emphasized.

The *chosson* followed his Rebbe's directives exactingly. The first thing on his agenda was to find a decent apartment, and during the next couple of days he spent all of his off-hours in this search. It turned out that the task was harder than he had anticipated. At the time, there was a shortage of rental units in Williamsburg; particularly in the immediate vicinity of the Stoliner Rebbe's house and *shul*, which were located in the heart of the neighborhood.

Finally, the *chosson* located an apartment that seemed to fit his needs perfectly, but the owner was not quite ready to rent it at the time. He had some doubts as to whether he would use it as an expansion of his own residence or put it on the rental market. He took down the *chosson's* telephone number and promised that should he decide to rent it, he would call him first. Upon returning, the *chosson* went to the Rebbe to brief him, and received his blessings for *brachah v'hatzlachah*.

Two weeks passed with no communication from the prospective landlord. The *chosson* had given up hope on the apartment and put it out of his mind. The wedding date was fast approaching, yet despite his disappointments regarding living quarters, the *chosson* did not succumb to pressure, maintaining his full-time learning schedule. One day, in middle of the morning session, several minutes before attending the *Rosh Yeshiva's* lecture, the *chosson* was suddenly called to appear in the Rebbe's study, which was adjacent to the yeshivah. He hurried to the Rebbe with anxious steps.

He had barely entered the room when the Rebbe asked him, "Did you find an apartment?"

"As yet, no. I'm really at a loss," he said with a worried tone.

"And what happened to the apartment you mentioned to me about two weeks ago?" the Rebbe asked.

"It seems that the man is not interested: two weeks have gone by and no one has been in touch with me. Generally, apartments in that area are rented within a day or two," the *chosson* explained.

"Listen to me," the Rebbe said with a firm tone. "Go to the man immediately, and ask about the status of the apartment. Find out if he has made up his mind whether or not to rent it."

With palpable hesitation and almost stuttering from uneasiness, the *chosson* blurted out, "But Rebbe, we are now in the middle of the first learning session. As a matter of fact, the *Rosh Yeshiva's* lecture is just about to begin."

"Our Sages tell us," the Rebbe responded, "that 'at times, refraining from performing something is the strengthening of that very thing.' Hurry, and with *Hashem's* help, you will be successful."

The *chosson* quickly strode to the apartment owner's home and asked about the status of the apartment.

"I'm truly delighted that you showed up at this moment," the man said. "You are lucky. Should you have arrived fifteen minutes later, the apartment would have been rented. Let me tell you what happened. When I finally made up my mind to rent it, I had totally forgotten about you. In the interim, another fellow was here, and ready to rent it immediately. He is scheduled to arrive in a quarter of an hour. Of course I will not rent it to him, since you were first."

After signing the lease agreement, the *chosson* returned to the yeshivah and shared the good news with his friends, commenting that when the Rebbe advised him to go in the middle of the session, he actually had been caught by surprise. For who was more scrupulous regarding Torah study than the Stoliner Rebbe, who made it a cardinal rule that adhering to learning sessions takes priority over everything else?

The profound consequence of *emunas chachomim* — a living demonstration of "*Viyaaminu baHashem ub'Moshe avdo;* and they had faith in Hashem and in Moshe, His servant" — crystallized in the *chosson's* mind.

"After what just happened, I now understand," he said elatedly. "Through the Rebbe's wisdom, I invested less than one hour at the right time, which saved me dozens of hours of aggravation and heartache. Above all, he saved me untold hours of *bitul Torah*."

The Significance of a Single Jew

Harav Chaim Shmulevitz

Rosh Yeshivah, Mirrer Yeshivah

The Significance of a Single Jew

Harav Chaim Shmulevitz zt"l, *Rosh Yeshivah of the Mirrer Yeshivah in Yerushalayim, was born in 5663/1903 in Stuchin, Poland where his father, Harav Alter Raphael, was* Rosh Yeshivah *of the yeshivah. The* tzaddik *"Reb Itzele Peterburger" (Rav Yitzchok Blazer, one of the most distinguished disciples of Rav Yisrael Salanter) served as* sandek *at his* bris *and blessed the infant with almost prophetic accuracy, saying that he would grow up to be one of the great luminaries of Torah and* mussar. *Indeed, he gained fame as a* wunderkind *who possessed an unusually sharp mind. In addition, his memory was so extraordinary that it was rumored that he did not know the meaning of forgetfulness.*

Despite his promising future, Chaim was forced to leave yeshivah at the age of 16 as a result of the sudden death of both of his parents. The burden of providing for his brother and two sisters rested entirely on his shoulders and he did not shirk the responsibility. During the day he was busy with commerce, and most of the nights he spent toiling in Torah.

The eminent Rosh Yeshivah, *Harav Shimon Shkop,* Rosh Yeshivah *of the yeshivah in Grodno, found out about this situation and was aghast that a student of Chaim's ability should be in the workforce instead of yeshivah. He immediately arranged for provisions for the orphans, and invited Chaim to join his yeshivah in Grodno. Within three short years, young Chaim was appointed to a lecturing post in the yeshivah. When Rav Shimon was asked if he could not find anyone as suitable as Chaim for the lecturing position, he replied, "Indeed there are many others who would qualify equally. But for the task of imbuing students with a true love of Torah, I did not find anyone who equals the " illuy [prodigy] of Stuchin."*

Reb Chaim continued his studies in Mir where the Rosh Yeshivah, *Harav Eliezer Yehuda Finkel, chose him as a suitable match for his outstanding daughter. With the outbreak of World War II, he remained with the Mirrer Yeshivah in its exile in Shanghai. Despite the trying conditions there, his dazzling Talmudic* shiurim *encouraged unparalleled effort in Torah study among the student body, exceeding the excitement in Torah study seen during tranquil times.*

After the war, he lived for a short while in America. With the establishment of the Mirrer Yeshivah in Yerushalayim, he immigrated to Eretz Yisrael *and served as its* Rosh Yeshivah. *His* shiurim *entranced his audiences, which included not only his own multitude of students but also the elite of the yeshivah world from throughout Israel. In his later years he also delivered* mussar *discourses that were published under the title* Sichos Mussar.

He passed away on 3 Teves, 6739/1979. More than 100,000 people attended his funeral. Today, his children and grandchildren are marbitzei Torah *of distinction.*

The *Mashgiach* of the Kamenitz Yeshivah in Yerushalayim, Harav Moshe Aaron Stern, related that he once attended the Bar Mitzvah of one of the students at the Kamenitz elementary school. The day of the Bar Mitzvah was one of freezing rain and heavy winds. The affair took place in the Katamon section of the city, quite a distance from other *Chareidi* neighborhoods.

When he arrived, he noticed a taxi pulling up, and heard the feeble voice of an elderly man asking for help in exiting from the car. Rav Stern rushed over and helped him. Once on the street, he discerned that the gentleman was walking to the hall with some difficulty. Suddenly, he realized that the elderly man was no other than Harav Chaim Shmulevitz, the eminent *Rosh Yeshivah* of the Mirrer Yeshivah.

That day happened to be a very taxing one for the *Rosh Yeshivah*. A memorial assembly had been held for Harav Mendel Zaks, in which Rav Chaim had been the keynote speaker. In addition, he had given his weekly Talmud lecture to the entire student body that evening, an exertion of mammoth proportions for a man whose very lifeblood was the exacting dissemination of Torah.

The Kamenitz *Mashgiach*, noticing the sheer fatigue of Rav Chaim, asked him why, after an especially exhausting day, he found it necessary to travel in inclement weather to attend the Bar Mitzvah.

"Let me explain it to you," Rav Chaim answered in a contemplative tone. "The Bar Mitzvah boy's father attends my *mussar* sessions regularly. I feel I owe him a debt of gratitude for his trouble in traveling weekly — in all weather conditions — from distant Katamon, just to hear my lecture. I feel that the proper thing for me to do is to reciprocate, disregarding the distance and the elements, and participate in his *simchah*."

"I beg the *Rosh Yeshivah's* pardon," the *Mashgiach* said, "but you are well aware that the crowds at the weekly *mussar shiur* are by far greater than the capacity of the auditorium. Whoever finds a seat considers himself a lucky man. Why do you feel a debt of gratitude to a person who participates in one of the most popular lectures in all of *Yerushalayim*?"

Rav Chaim explained that our Sages' explanation of wealth, whereby "a penny and another penny ... add up to a large sum," is also valid regarding people: a crowd is merely an aggregation of many individuals, and if we overlook the significance of the single *Yid*, we have disregarded the entire crowd.

"You must view this in the right perspective," Rav Chaim explained. "Imagine if the father of the Bar Mitzvah boy would not participate, and then another and yet another person would ignore my lectures. To whom would I deliver my *mussar* message? Every single participant makes it possible for the lecture to happen, and each one adds to the atmosphere of *yiras Shomayim*. Should that not be cause enough for paying them a minimum debt of gratitude, by attending their *simchos*?" he asked rhetorically.

The Refund

Harav Yisroel Friedman

Boyaner-Leipziger Rebbe

The Refund

Harav Yisroel Friedman zt"l, the Boyaner-Leipziger
Rebbe, was born in 5638/1878. His father was
known as the Pachad Yitzchok, and was the son of
the first Sadigura Rebbe, Harav Avrohom Yaakov,
son of Harav Yisrael of Ruzhin. He received his
early education from master educators and noted
Chassidic thinkers handpicked and supervised by
his father.

In 5677/1917 Yisrael's father passed away. As
a result of the First World War, many of his father's
Chassidim relocated to Germany. Reb Yisrael was
invited to Leipzig to head this budding Chassidic
community. Although operating in a culture alien
to his upbringing, he was successful in injecting the
joy and enthusiasm of Chassidus into the hearts of
many of the city's inhabitants. One of the most
appreciated accomplishments of the Rebbe was
the establishment of a modern mikvah, making
kedushas Yisrael that much more attractive to the
German Jewish population.

The city of Leipzig was noted for generations as
an international marketing hub with a variety of
annual trade shows for an array of industries. These
business opportunities drew Jewish businessmen
from many countries. Transient businessmen, along

with the local followers of the Rebbe, formed a
solid core for the community, giving it an
international tone.

Just before the outbreak of World War II, he was
successful in escaping the clutches of the Nazis. He
immigrated to Eretz Yisrael, and settled in Tel Aviv.
There, he served his Creator quietly and without
fanfare, creating an island of holiness in this
tumultuous metropolis, despite his afflictions with
disease and chronic fatigue.

He passed away on the first day of Rosh Chodesh
Elul, 5711/1951 and was put to his eternal rest in
Tzfas. His Torah and good deeds remain as his
perpetual memorial.

Following the passing of the Boyaner-Leipziger Rebbe, his family found among his possessions an envelope with a substantial amount of money in it. On the envelope was written: "Upon my passage to the world of eternity, kindly deliver this envelope to _____, residing in Tel Aviv." That individual was by no means a Chassid of the Rebbe, but did visit on a regular basis.

In addition to the money, the envelope also contained a brief note written in the Rebbe's handwriting, explaining the reason for his request:

The person had a habit of coming to me from time to time with a kvitl and pidyon.[1] He constantly beseeched me about a specific problem, which was heavy on his heart.

---

1. It is customary among Chassidim that when visiting their Rebbe on a formal basis, they enumerate all family members on a piece of paper which includes an outline of their request. The paper is called a *kvitl* and is usually accompanied with a donation, called a *pidyon.*

Right from his first visit, I realized that as far as that specific matter is concerned, I am in no position to help him. Nevertheless, in order not to deflate his hopes and risk the possibility of a resultant depression, I accepted the pidyon and offered him my sincere blessing that if it is the will of Hashem, *his request will surely be answered.*

When he would leave my house, I always placed the pidyon *in a special drawer for safekeeping. Since, in reality, I knew that I was helpless in solving his problem, I planned that eventually, at the appropriate time, the money would be returned to him. I beseech you, my close ones, to kindly respect my wishes and return the money to its rightful owner.*

Immersion in Torah
Saved His Life

Harav Moshe Feinstein

Rosh Yeshivah,
Tiferes Yerushalayim

Immersion in Torah
Saved His Life

Harav Moshe Feinstein zt"l was born on 7 Adar 5655/1895 in the town of Uzda, Russia. He was named Moshe after Moshe Rabbeinu, *as he was born on* Moshe Rabbeinu's *birthday and yahrzeit. In his youth, he learned mostly from his father, Harav Dovid, who was Rav of the town and one of the outstanding disciples of the Netziv of Volozhin. He was also a disciple of Harav Isser Zalman Meltzer,* Rosh Yeshivah *of Slutzk, and Harav Pesach Pruskin, whom he considered his primary Torah guide.*

When his father ascended to the position of Rav of Starubin, Rav Moshe was asked to take the place of his father as Rav of Uzda, despite his young age of 20. In 5680/1920, he assumed the rabbinical position of Lubon, a city with a large population of Torah scholars. This was a most turbulent and chaotic era in Russia and the country was in a state of anarchy. Rav Moshe had been in his new post barely one year when he was forced to escape a horrific pogrom in Lubon.

The worst was yet to come. In 5690/1930 the Bolsheviks established a branch of the notorious Yevsektzia, a Jewish division of the Communist regime that sought to eradicate every vestige of the Jewish faith. Hundreds of religious functionaries of the region — rabbis, scribes and cantors — were either imprisoned or banished to the Gulags. In those anguished days, the magnificence of Rav Moshe emerged. Like a devoted shepherd to his flock, he nursed the wounds of the terrorized Jewish community while at the same time attending to his normal rabbinical responsibilities, responding to voluminous halachic and congregational inquiries from all parts of Russia.

When the situation deteriorated further, making it impossible to stay on, he immigrated to the United States. Upon his arrival in 5696/1936, he began lecturing at Mesifta Tiferes Yerushalayim. There he taught Torah to thousands of students for close to half a century. Many of his devoted disciples took positions of leadership in the rabbinate and in education throughout the United States. He left his mark on American Orthodoxy as the leading Torah authority, as reflected in his eight-volume masterpiece of halachic responsa, Igros Moshe.

Rav Moshe's golden character was truly exceptional. A most fitting description of his personality is the expression "הי עניו הי חסיד מתלמידיו של אהרן הכהן" — "…very humble and very pious — from the disciples of Aaron HaKohen." Like Aaron HaKohen, his very essence was peace loving and kindness. Notwithstanding his encyclopedic knowledge of all areas of Torah — it is said that he reviewed the entire Shulchan Aruch with all of its commentaries over four hundred times during his lifetime — his humble demeanor was so profound that every individual, including children, always felt comfortable in his company. He never kept a grudge against a fellow Jew, despite prevailing controversies. Whoever came in contact with him came away inspired by his warmth and empathy, for he was a living example of kiddush Hashem, the sanctification of G-d's Name.

He passed away on 13 Adar, 5746/1986. It is estimated that approximately a quarter of a million people attended the funeral processions in New York and Yerushalayim. He left behind a generation of Torah scholars and educators who continue to uphold his standards of excellence.

Harav Moshe Feinstein was one of the last highly respected rabbonim to leave the Soviet Union. Despite the unremitting harassment of the Communist government, he continued to lead his congregation in Lubon and to respond to a huge volume of halachic questions from throughout Russia for close to twenty years. After he came to America, he was once asked the reason for delaying his departure for so long, at a time when almost all other rabbis had left. Rav Moshe answered, in his typically direct style, that for the very reason that they left, he remained. "I realized that throughout my entire region not one *Rav* competent in Jewish law and jurisprudence remained. If I too emigrated, the region would be abandoned. Only when the situation became absolutely unbearable, I realized that staying on would not help the Jews. At that point, I could leave." That critical moment arrived in 5696/1936. Rav Moshe made various attempts to secure an exit visa from the government, but was consistently turned down. Realizing that an imminent threat to his life was looming and that the virulent anti-Semitic local authorities were bent on blocking his departure, he decided to try his luck in Moscow, where some of his friends had contacts with the appropriate governmental agencies. The big hurdle, however, was to get to Moscow — not a simple task. Even within Russia, an internal passport was required for travel, and that relatively minor document was not forthcoming.

Rav Moshe came upon a novel plan. Disguising himself as a Russian peasant who would not arouse suspicion, he successfully evaded the authorities and arrived in the capital. Checking into a hotel was out of the question, since by law all travelers were required to have their identity cards stamped by the local police, authorizing their stay. However, he had *siyata d'Shmaya* — Divine assistance: immediately upon his arrival he was able to rent a room from a non-Jew who was ready to forgo all legal formalities, despite the dangers. He remained in Moscow for several weeks, subsisting on potatoes and water. Part of the day he was busy procuring the required documents, and the rest of the time he spent in a local *beis medrash*, toiling in Torah.

One day, Rav Moshe became so engrossed in a complex Talmudic subject that he lost track of time, not realizing that most of the night had passed. He decided that considering the lateness of the hour, it did not pay to retire to his lodgings. Instead, he spent the balance of the night learning in the *shul*. In the morning, after *Shacharis*, he returned to his quarters, apologizing to the owner for not returning for the night.

"You apologize? Are you aware what great miracle happened to both of us last night?" the owner asked with palpable emotion. "In the early evening hours, secret service agents encircled the district in pursuit of undocumented residents. They went from house to house and it was impossible to escape them. Many people were hauled off to headquarters, and I need not tell you what awaits them there. Your absence saved both of us from long prison sentences, or worse."

It is noteworthy, that even after leaving Russia under conditions of *pikuach nefesh* — clear danger to life — Rav Moshe seriously doubted whether he was justified in his decision to leave. When he met Harav Elchonon Wasserman in 5699/1939, during the latter's visit to America on behalf of his yeshivah in Baranovitch, Rav Moshe presented him with his dilemma, which rested heavily on his conscience. He was finally placated only upon hearing Rav Elchonon quote from his illustrious *rebbe*, the Chofetz Chaim: a country such as Russia, where *Hashem's* name is banned, is considered like a lavatory, where according to *halachah* one may not engage in Torah study. "It is impossible for a human being to live his life closeted in a lavatory," Rav Elchonon stated categorically. "Your decision was absolutely correct."

A Parallel Experience

In 5754/1994 this author visited an elderly Torah sage, Harav Boruch Halevi Leizerovski, a disciple of the holy Chofetz Chaim. Indeed, I was most captivated by the firsthand anecdotes he related. At the time he was close to 90 years old, yet as sharp as a tack. After relating one story after another of his great *rebbe*, he stopped, obviously out of anecdotes he had personally witnessed.

"Frankly, I do not have any more personal stories about the Chofetz Chaim, however I invite you to listen to a story relating to myself."

I must admit that, at the time, I was taken aback, disinclined to hear the rabbi's own life's experiences. But after hearing his story, I was awestruck. His tale underscores manifest *hashgachah pratis* that places a person in a specific time and place to enable his rescue:

"Several years before World War II, I was appointed *Rav* of a Lithuanian *shul* in Lodz, Poland. When the war broke out, I was shipped to Auschwitz and was among the few who survived three full years in that most bloodsoaked of all human habitats. Upon arrival, all inmates underwent the "*selektzia*" — selection by the inhuman beast, Dr. Mengele. With a minor indication of his finger, he indicated who would live and who would die. Like hundreds of thousands before me, I passed by and, as a healthy young man, was directed to the right — the work brigade, rather than to the gas chambers.

"Close to three horrifying years followed, years of indescribable pain and anguish. Then, as the war was winding down to its final end, we were told that our group had to pass Dr. Mengele again. By now, we all understood its meaning, having been educated with blood and tears in the definition of that most dreadful word in the entire dictionary, *selektzia*: the weakest among us would perish, while the fate of those appearing in better health would be postponed until the next *selektzia*.

"At the time I was suffering from an abscessed wound at the heel of my foot causing extreme pain with every step I took. Upon reaching that beast, I controlled myself with an iron will from displaying any pain, making my passage with a normal stride. He did not discern my agony and motioned me to the right.

"Not a moment passed and I realized what a terrible mistake I had made and was overtaken with deep remorse. Memory flashes came back to me from the first moment the Nazis marched into Lodz and the atrocities they carried out, acts that are simply unfathomable to a normal human being. At that time, I became convinced beyond doubt that what I was witnessing was a Heavenly decree, the likes of which we as a nation have never experienced throughout our two millennia of martyrdom. I vowed that I would not make any attempts toward my survival, relying instead on His guidance and His dictates wherever that would lead.

"*Have I suddenly become clever, deciding my own destiny?*" I said to myself. No, I made up my mind firmly! *Hashem*, who has guided me these last three years without the slightest planning on my part, will follow me through to wherever I'm destined to be, either among the survivors or among the martyrs.

"Surprising as it may sound, I eluded the guards and sneaked back into the line of people about to pass Mengele. This time around, when I passed by, I did not camouflage any of my symptoms, not even the facial contortions associated with my painful walk. Needless to say, he motioned me to the left, together with a group of sick and infirm inmates.

"None of us had to be told where we were headed. The brutal facts of life in Auschwitz had taught us all too well what to expect. I, like the other religious members of the group, began to prepare for our last passage, the imminent crossing of that fateful bridge into eternity.

"And here I learned firsthand the meaning of those propitious words written thousands of years ago in *sefer Tehillim*: 'מה גדלו מעשיך ה' מאד עמקו מחשבותיך' — 'How great are Your deeds, *Hashem*; exceedingly profound are Your thoughts.' 'איש בער לא ידע וכסיל לא יבין את זאת' — 'A boor cannot know, nor can a fool understand this.'

"The infirm and I were not taken to the gas chambers! Rather, we were loaded onto trucks and taken to a modern hospital in the Auschwitz compound that the Nazis had built for one specific purpose, to dupe the International Red Cross into believing that the Germans provided outstanding medical attention to their prisoners.

"I spent close to two weeks in the hospital in the care of some of the finest, world-class Jewish physicians. They attended to my foot and largely restored my general well-being. Some time later, I found out that the entire group that was directed to the right side was ordered to participate in the 'death marches.' These marches were so named since the objective was to cause as much mortality as possible. At the final stage of the war, when the Nazis realized that the end was nearing, they ordered the last remnants of the concentration camps, including Auschwitz, to march daily tens of kilometers aimlessly, with almost no food or drink. To our great misfortune, the vast majority perished, may *Hashem* avenge their blood."

Rav Leizerovski ended with this last note. "Imagine what would have happened to me had I ended up on the right side, with the relatively healthy ones. With my ailing foot I could not have survived even half a day of those marches. Seeing to it that I was reclassified as sick was *Hashem's* method of saving my life."

Courage of the Faithful

Harav Yaakov Landa

Rav of Bnei Brak

Courage of the Faithful

Harav Yaakov Landa zt"l, Rav of Bnei Brak, was born in 5653/1893 in Kurnitz, Russia. His father, Rav Moshe Leib, was a scion of the eminent Noda BiYehuda and served as Rav of the town. In his youth, Yaakov studied in the Lubavitch Yeshivah in Rostow and gained fame for his outstanding diligence and comprehensive knowledge. He was ordained by the world-renowned genius, the Gaon of Rogatchov, Harav Yosef Rosen, who lovingly referred to him as "my young Torah sage."

Escaping conscription into the Soviet army, he was welcomed by the Rebbe of Lubavitch, Harav Sholom Ber Schneerson, who appointed him "Court Rabbi" with responsibility for all halachic issues of the household. He relocated to Moscow after the Bolshevik Revolution. The authorities strictly enforced a law outlawing "parasites"— people who, in their view, were not productive. To comply with the law, he turned to a local shoemaker, seeking to serve as his apprentice. The man looked up and saw Rav Yaakov with his aristocratic deportment and patriarchal beard, and commented: "You should not fix soles; you are more suitable to fix Jewish souls." The simpleton's words penetrated deep into his heart, and with the blessing of his Rebbe, he commenced on his new career, fixing Jewish souls.

He began by organizing groups of Jewish university students who, due to a combination of factors, could not attend yeshivah. He taught them Torah and gave them the personal attention and warmth they so craved. It is no wonder that his influence was truly out of the ordinary.

In 5695/1935 he immigrated to Eretz Yisrael, and by recommendation of the Chazon Ish was appointed Rav of the city of Bnei Brak, which was then in its early stages. As Rav he gained a reputation as an uncompromising, tough supervisor regarding all aspects of religious behavior of the city. His kashrus apparatus gained respect throughout the entire world, second to none in its high standards. The sanctity of Shabbos and of modesty, as well as the mitzvos relating to agriculture, were high on his priority list. Much of what Bnei Brak is today could be credited to his vigilance and devotion.

He passed away on 25 Shevat, 5746/1986 in his ninety-third year of life. His son was appointed as his successor in the rabbinate of Bnei Brak.

Harav Yaakov Landa was known for his utter fearlessness in all areas pertaining to *Yiddishkeit.* There are numerous stories of the daring incidents of his youth, years before his immigration to *Eretz Yisrael.*

When he was 18, Rav Yaakov received a draft notice from the Russian army, despite the fact that he occupied a rabbinical position, which should have exempted him. Fearing that he would be forced into situations where his religion might be compromised, he fled, hiding at the court of his Rebbe, Harav Sholom Ber of Lubavitch. The Rebbe appointed him as the official court *Rav*, authorizing him to adjudicate all halachic questions directed to him by his Chassidim as well as those arising in the Rebbe's own household. He continued at his post even after Rav Sholom Ber's passing, when his son Harav Yosef Yitzchok ascended to the leadership of Lubavitch.

One day, a short while after Harav Yosef Yitzchok took over the leadership of *Chabad*, the notorious Russian secret police encircled the Rebbe's house. In truth, it was not all that uncommon an occurrence, as many a religious leader experienced midnight raids by those uninvited guests.

A high-ranking officer, escorted by armed soldiers, burst into the house and howled angrily: "No one should dare move from his place." Everyone in the household, including the Rebbe, knew well that the objective of the visit was to make a thorough search of the premises for one purpose: to find anything deemed subversive or counterrevolutionary and use it as a pretext for arrest and imprisonment.

At the time, there was a secret memorandum on the Rebbe's desk in his study that graphically highlighted the pain and suffering of the Jewish population in Russia, imploring all freedom-loving people to exert their influence and protest against those brutalities. The memorandum was entitled "קומה ישראל ממנוחתך" — "Arise, O Israel, From Your Passivity."

The Rebbe's family was dumbfounded and in absolute shock, knowing well that the moment the secret police, the infamous N.K.V.D., would enter the study they would find more incriminating material than they could ever have hoped for. The "*Kumah*" ["Arise"] memorandum would surely constitute treason, as it slandered the Soviet regime.

Uncharacteristic of his usual calm demeanor, the Rebbe himself was in a state of great anxiety, which surprised and alarmed the household members. *This is not the first time the house is being searched by the police*, they thought, *yet despite the intimidation and constant danger, the Rebbe has always maintained his widespread network of* Yiddishkeit. *Why is he suddenly so afraid?*

What they did not realize was that this time the entire Jewish community would be exposed by the document now resting on the Rebbe's desk. If it fell into the hands of the government, the consequences would be collective. The only one who was unruffled was young Rav Yaakov. Despite the imminent danger, he somehow managed to sneak into the Rebbe's study, remove the document and hide it in a safe place.

Having accomplished this mission, he walked nonchalantly into the parlor where the Rebbe and his family stood, as though he had just become aware of their distinguished visitors. While soldiers and plainclothesmen rummaged through the house, he managed to whisper four key words: "The '*Kumah*' is safe."

Instantaneously, the Rebbe's complexion and his usually happy countenance returned to normal. The search ended uneventfully, like all preceding ones; no incriminating data had been found.

Rav Yaakov's daring and courage saved the Rebbe, and indirectly tens of thousands of Russian Jews, during this dark era of Bolshevik rule.

A Precious Gift From Hashem

Harav
Yechezkel
Levenstein

Mashgiach Ponevizh Yeshivah

A Precious Gift
From Hashem

Harav Yechezkel Levenstein zt"l, Mashgiach of the Ponevizh Yeshivah, was born in 5644/1884 in Warsaw, Poland. His father, Rav Yehuda was a scion of the legendary Tosfos Yom Tov. Yechezkel's mother passed away when he was only 5. The family subsisted in dismal poverty. When he was 13, his father sent him to work in a flower shop to help alleviate the household's financial burden. The young boy worked hard and earned well.

A major turning point of his life occurred one Friday while in the mikvah, when his entire week's earnings were stolen from him. The incident had a profound impact on the impressionable youngster. After considerable soul-searching, he concluded that if a week's hard-earned wages can so easily vanish, it must be that life's purpose is not the accumulation of more and more physical wealth. Rather, one should work at serving Hashem, the earnings of which no one can remove. Immediately after Shabbos he left for the Yeshiva of Radin. The influence of the holy Chofetz Chaim and that of Harav Yerucham Levovitz (the yeshivah's Mashgiach at the time) had a lifelong impact on him. Eventually, Rav Yerucham sent him to the famed Kelm Talmud Torah where he grew in both Torah knowledge and refinement of character.

When he reached marriageable age, several affluent matches were proposed. He declined all exterior virtues and married someone from a poor, simple background who was imbued with overflowing yiras Shomayim *and whose objective coincided with his: total dedication of one's life to the service of* Hashem.

When World War I broke out and all Lithuanian yeshivos *relocated to central Russia away from the devastation of the war, Rav Yechezkel was appointed* Mashgiach *of the Kletzk Yeshivah. From there, he moved to* Eretz Yisrael *to become* Mashgiach *of the recently formed Lomza Yeshivah in Petach Tikvah. After a short while, however, he was urged to move back to Mir, Lithuania, due the sudden passing of its illustrious* Mashgiach, *Rav Yerucham Levovitz.*

During the Holocaust, while all Torah institutions in Europe were doomed to annihilation, the only yeshivah that was destined to survive was the Mirrer Yeshivah. Through an extraordinary set of miracles, the entire yeshivah escaped to Shanghai, China. For six long years, hundreds of students grew immeasurably in Torah and yiras Shomayim, *despite enormous obstacles — not the least of which was the knowledge that their families in Europe were being tormented, dehumanized and killed with unparalleled brutality. Their superhuman accomplishments would have been impossible, if not for Rav Yechezkel, who infused inspiration, hope, integrity and virtue into every aspect of the yeshivah's existence.*

When the war ended, he spent some time in America. In 5714/1954, at the age of 70, he was invited to join the Ponevizh Yeshivah in Bnei Brak as its Mashgiach. *For two full decades he motivated and educated thousands of students who, following his example, resolved to dedicate their lives to Torah.*

He passed away on 18 Adar, 5734/1974 at age 90, leaving behind a wonderful generation of Torah scholars and educators in Eretz Yisrael *and America.*

Harav Yechezkel Levenstein's manner in *avodas Hashem* was to accentuate the fear of G-d. Humor, therefore, was not his forte; even a fleeting light statement was rare.

In his later years, a student once entered his study and noticed his *rebbe* in a most uncharacteristic, cheerful disposition. It was a remarkable sight, so much so that he gathered the courage to ask Rav Yechezkel directly regarding his unusual behavior.

The *rebbe* answered blissfully. "Years before the war, when I was appointed as *Mashgiach* of the Mirrer Yeshivah in Europe, my salary was set at a certain amount per month. It was merely a pittance, not sufficing even for basic expenses. What's more, it never arrived with any regularity, as the yeshivah's financial state was most pathetic.

"How, you may wonder, did my family manage? I prayed to *Hashem* with sincerity that He show me His compassion and provide for my family, so that they not suffer starvation. Simultaneously, I worked hard to develop the trait of *bitachon* — absolute faith in *Hashem.* ברוך הוא וברוך שמו, I am forever grateful to Him for having provided for my family throughout all those years. Despite our extreme poverty, we were all fed and clothed and maintained ourselves in good health.

"Years passed, and during the war my family was fortunate enough to be saved from annihilation, together with the entire Mirrer Yeshivah, in Shanghai. The support of the yeshivah was entirely dependent on contributions from America, which at the time was in a state of war with Japan (which controlled Shanghai), so all money transfers had to be done circuitously. Any direct contact with the United States was considered treasonous and punishable by long prison terms.

"Needless to say, our livelihood did not improve by any means; in fact, for months on end we received almost no salary at all. How did we continue to survive? Exactly as we had in Mir, with prayers and *Tehillim*, seasoned with the *Shaar HaBitachon*, the "Chapter on Reliance" [on *Hashem*] of the classic *Chovos Halevovos*.

"After the war, the Ponevizh Rav, Harav Yosef Kahaneman, invited me to join the staff of his yeshivah as *Mashgiach*. With his generous spirit, he offered me a hefty salary, compared to what I was earning at the time. For a long time the checks arrived promptly.

"During that period of time, a gradual ebbing of my *bitachon*, my sole reliance on Hashem, began; a change of which I myself wasn't even aware. Slowly, gradually, I began to de-emphasize *bitachon*, subconsciously assuming that I was on safe ground and did not have to focus on financial sustenance in my prayers.

"Of late, our yeshivah is undergoing some cash-flow problems, as a result of the massive expansion of its campus. For several months now, I haven't received a salary check. Today, during my prayers a truly beautiful thing happened to me. Suddenly, realizing my vulnerability, my mind began focusing on *bitachon*, and I beseeched *Hashem* to answer my supplications and help me support my family. Today's prayer was of the same quality as in the olden days, full of heart and soul and full of faith in Him.

"Receiving back this great gift, *bitachon* in Hashem without any intermediaries or false assurances, is a phenomenal gift! I treasure it immensely, and that is why my spirits rose so high today!"

Respect for a Guest

Harav
Yisrael
Abuchatzera

The Baba Sali

Respect for a Guest

Harav Yisrael Abuchatzera zt"l, the "Baba Sali," was born in Morocco in the year 5650/1890. His father was the eminent Rav Masod. From his youth he strove to develop purity and holiness in his daily life, and he was most scrupulous not to tarnish his eyes with licentious sights. Even as a young man, his reputation spread and multitudes flocked to him to receive his blessing. He was reverentially called "Baba Sali," which in Arabic denotes "the praying father."

In 5681/1921 he visited Eretz Yisrael. *Notwithstanding his youth, he was received by the Torah sages there with singular respect. Even the* Saba Kadisha *[Holy Elder], Harav Shlomo Eliezer Alfandri, who was approximately 100 years old at the time, requested the young man's blessing, stating that he did not know anyone with more* yiras Shomayim *than the Baba Sali.*

He immigrated to Eretz Yisrael *in 5711/1951 and settled in the Negev town of Netivot. Established there, he drew tens of thousands of people from all segments of the population – Ashkenazic and Sephardic; Chassidic and Lithuanian; Chareidi and secular. All flocked to his sacred dwelling, knowing that he was a living personification of holiness and spirituality.*

He passed away in his 90's on 4 Shevat, 5744/1984 and was put to rest in Netivot. Tens of thousands gather at his gravesite on the day of his yahrzeit. He left behind a wonderful family who continue in his footsteps.

Harav Yisrael Abuchatzera, the "Baba Sali," had a distinctive style in performing the *mitzvah* of *hachnossas orchim*, welcoming guests. Millionaire and pauper alike, everyone passing through the door was offered food and drink, from the early morning hours till after midnight. These were not just meals; they were sumptuous repasts, served in royal style with variety that even the rich were not accustomed to on a daily basis.

Despite the substantial costs involved — and though he himself lived a most humble, minimal existence — the Baba Sali was not ready to part with this custom; wishing to bestow upon his guests the blessing of abundance and prosperity.

Once on *erev* Rosh Hashanah, in late afternoon he asked one of his associates to go to Yeshivat Hanegev, in Netivot, and summon a student who occasionally served as his driver.

The young man rushed over to the Baba Sali's house. The hour was 6:30 p.m. and it was already Yom Tov by the time he arrived. To his great surprise, he found everyone, including family members and guests, sitting around the table, ready for *Kiddush.*

When he heard that the reason he was called was that the Baba Sali wished to extend a personal invitation to him to join his Rosh Hashanah meal, the boy felt both honored and stunned. He was totally cognizant of the fact that there were numerous drivers who graciously offered their services and considered it a rare *z'chus* to be given the privilege. He felt he was not the giver, but the recipient of the favor, with no need for the Baba Sali to show appreciation or reciprocity.

After thanking him for the great honor, the youth remarked that though he would have loved to attend, he had to nevertheless decline the offer since he customarily *davened* in the yeshivah at a much later hour than the general synagogues. Rav Yisrael urged him, however, to please come and eat the Yom Tov meal as his guest immediately after *davening*, regardless of the hour.

The lad left the house and went to the yeshivah. There, they were not even close to beginning the prayers: the yeshivah scholars were busy getting ready for the upcoming new year with thorough spiritual preparations, including the recitation of *Tehillim* and the learning of *mussar*. After that, the service itself took a great deal of time due to the intensity of the *davening*. When the boy finally arrived at the Baba Sali's home, the hour was close to nine o'clock.

Once inside, the boy could barely believe what he saw. All the members of the household, including the guests, were sitting at the table in the exact positions he had left them hours before. It was revealed later that the Baba Sali felt that since he had extended the invitation to the student, he had an obligation to include him in the family meal and not leave him to eat alone. He therefore held up the Yom Tov meal for over two hours so that he would comply with the verse מוצא שפתיך תשמור — 'You should fulfill the utterances of your mouth,' in its fullest, most absolute sense.

Displaying great sensitivity, Rav Yisrael showered the student with attention throughout the meal. He was concerned that the boy might feel ill at ease over the fact that he was responsible for the extended delay. To assuage these feelings, the Baba Sali made it a point to display love to him, as if he were his own child.

Spared By His Tzidkus

Harav
Avrohom
Abba
Leifer
Pittsburgher Rebbe

Spared by His Tzidkus

Harav Avrohom Abba Leifer zt"l, the Pittsburgher Rebbe, was born in 5678/1918 in Krula, Hungary. His father was Harav Yosef, son of the famous Rav Mordche'le of Nadvorna.

When Rav Yosef's brother passed away at a young age, he left his wife and a large household of children. Rav Yosef traveled to America, where it would be easier to put together the necessary funds to help the widow and orphans. Upon reaching Pittsburgh, Pennsylvania, he found many devoted Orthodox Jews who were seeking inspiration and warmth. They found those qualities in their European guest and they beseeched him to stay. He relocated his family there, serving as the Chassidic Rebbe of Pittsburgh.

In his concern for the education of his children, he and his devoted wife sent their three sons back to Hungary to learn in various yeshivos. Rav Avrohom Abba was sent to Rachov and excelled in his studies to the degree that the Rosh Yeshivah, *Harav Shlomo Zalman Friedman, granted him rabbinical ordination at the young age of 17. The famous Reb Issomor'l of Nadvorna recognized his outstanding qualities and chose him as his son-in-law.*

During the Second World War, the three Leifer boys could not leave Europe, and two of them perished in the Holocaust. The only survivor was Rav Avrohom Abba. Three years after the war, he finally was able to leave Communist Romania and return to his parents in America, whom he had not seen for seventeen years. He settled in Newark, New Jersey, and in 5726/1966, after his father's passing, moved to Pittsburgh to fill the position of Pittsburgher Rebbe.

Rav Avrohom Abba always felt strong emotional ties to the Holy Land. After several years in Pittsburgh, he moved to Eretz Yisroel. He settled in the port city of Ashdod, where for the final two decades of his life he illuminated the city with his heartfelt prayers and special spiritual qualities. His Shabbos tish attracted large crowds of people who wished to lift their Shabbos experience to higher planes.

He passed away on 10 Teves, 5730/1970. His son was elected to succeed him in leading the "Pittsburgh" Chassidic community of Ashdod.

When the Nazis marched into Chernowitz, they immediately set off their reign of terror and anti-Semitic campaign. The Jews were herded into the confines of a ghetto and the threat of deportation and extermination loomed over them.

One Thursday, a Jew arrived at the house of Harav Issomor'l Rosenbaum, the Nadvorna Rebbe, to seek his advice about a matter of life-and-death. As he was leaving, the Rebbe's son-in-law, Harav Avrohom Abba Leifer, escorted him out to the street, wishing him much success in coping with the situation.

At the time, the Nazis had already instituted the notorious edict forcing all Jews to wear the yellow Star of David for immediate identification. Rav Avrohom Abba was engrossed in the visitor's problems, forgetting that he had stepped outside without wearing the yellow tag. To his misfortunate, a Nazi officer spotted him and immediately took him into custody.

His wife, who happened to look out of the window, watched the entire scene but was helpless to intercede on his behalf. She did however gather the courage to run out and, despite the imminent danger, give him his *tallis* and *tefillin* and two small *challos*, so that he would have *lechem mishnah* for Shabbos.

Arriving at the detention center, and realizing that he was the only one who was still wearing a beard, he stationed himself facing the wall so as not to draw attention to himself. He spent his entire time *davening* and reciting *Tehillim* with great passion.

Friday morning, a Nazi officer assembled all the prisoners and announced that within two days special trains would arrive to take them to a work camp. "There you will finally normalize, living productive lives, not your lazy, parasitic Jewish existence, preying on the gentile population," he snarled.

We can well imagine the anxiety and trepidation of the poor Jews in that squalid detention camp. By then, most, if not all, had heard of the horrors and barbaric tortures inflicted on Polish Jews in the work camps. Rav Avrohom Abba spent the entire Shabbos in prayer and supplication to our Father in Heaven to demonstrate mercy to His chosen people, delivering them from the imminent calamity. He did not however alter his customary Shabbos mode, conducting himself with happiness and joy, singing all traditional *z'miros*, as if he were with his family on a Shabbos in his prewar home.

Sunday arrived, a day of reckoning of momentous proportions, for on this day the fate of the entire group would be sealed to die or to live. The trains arrived and the Jewish prisoners were crammed into them, to be taken to an unknown destination, a place that would eventually go down in history as the most iniquitous habitat on Earth: Auschwitz.

As the Jews were being shoved through the train's doors, a Nazi tapped Rav Avrohom Abba on his shoulder, motioning him to step aside. "I had no doubt in my mind that since I was the only one in the group with a beard and *payos*, he had picked me as the victim for a sadistic workout," Rav Avrohom Abba later commented.

"I thought to myself that if I am destined to die now, at least I will have had the *z'chus* to pass to eternity with the profile of a *Yid*, the age-old Jewish *Tzelem Elokim*." [In Kabbalistic literature, the beard is of great significance, as it symbolizes 'G-d's image.']

Slowly, the station emptied of its Jews, who were unfortunately deported to Auschwitz, except for Rav Avrohom Abba. The officer turned to him and said, "I've been observing you now for the past three days. I noticed that you were the only one among the entire group whose behavior was in keeping with the standards I expected from a true spiritual leader. I decided to save you, despite the danger it poses to me. You may now go back to the ghetto."

Upon returning home, he was welcomed by everyone with the blessing ברוך אתה ה' מחיה המתים — "Blessed are You, G-d... Who has brought the dead back to life."

Rav Avrohom Abba held special regard for those who had suffered during the Holocaust. Following his sojourn in America, where he became known as the Pittsburgher Rebbe, he moved to Ashdod in *Eretz Yisroel*. One day, a wealthy man who had great appreciation for the Rebbe's accomplishments came to see him. He offered to finance the construction of a new synagogue as well as a yeshivah with dormitory facilities, stipulating but one rather "minor" request: that the Rebbe promise to divide with him his share in *Gan Eden* and include him in his abode there.

The Rebbe went into deep meditation for several minutes, as if in a trance. Finally, he replied reflectively, "I am more than ready to share with you the Torah that I have learned, as the Sages have taught that the supporter of Torah splits the reward with the one actually studying Torah. However, your request to share my place in *Gan Eden* is a totally different matter. Our Sages have taught that those who have died for the sake of sanctifying G-d's Name are in a class all their own, where no one else has access.

"You must understand," he continued, "that this also includes the Holocaust survivors, for they too were tormented with deathly pain and suffering which has put them in an exclusive category. I'm afraid you will have to withdraw your second stipulation."

The Z'chus of Survivors

After living in Yerushalayim for about a year's time, the Satmar Rebbe, Harav Yoel Teitelbaum, decided to relocate to America. One day, a guest came knocking on his door — Rav Osher Zelig Margulius, one of the most prominent Torah sages of the city. He had heard about the Rebbe's impending move, and he came personally to dissuade him from going through with his decision.

"Our Rebbe, our leader," he addressed the Satmar Rebbe, "in whose care will you be leaving us, should you move to America? If G-d forbid someone will face a misfortune, whom will he have to turn to?" he asked.

"Let me give you some practical advice," the Rebbe said pensively. "If anyone will be seeking a blessing that will have an impact in Heaven, all he has to do is go to a *shul* and keep his eyes open during *Shacharis*. When the congregants roll up their sleeves to place the *tefillin* on their forearms, watch for a person displaying a tattooed number engraved into his flesh.

"That is the person to whom you should turn, for after having gone through that purgatory, he was so totally cleansed and purified that his blessing surely has great weight in the Heavenly court."

Never Give Up Hope

Harav
Yitzchok
Zev
Soloveitchik

Rav of Brisk

Never Give Up Hope

Harav Yitzchok Zev Soloveitchik zt"l, *Rav of Brisk,*
was born in 5647/1887. His father, the illustrious
Rav Chaim Brisker was the son of Rav Yosef Ber, a
scion of Harav Chaim Volozhiner (the great disciple
of the Vilna Gaon). Throughout his youth, Yitzchok
Zev's father spent many hours daily as his teacher,
until his passing in 5678/1918.

When he was approximately 30, Rav Yitzchok Zev
was chosen to fill his late father's position as Rav of
the great city of Brisk, one of the most prestigious
rabbinical positions in Eastern Europe. He did not
disappoint his electorate, immediately leaping into a
plethora of activities to strengthen the religious fiber
of the city. His intelligence and good judgment were
legendary and within a short time he had gained a
reputation as an outstanding Torah leader and
community organizer.

Rav Yitzchok Zev did not head a yeshivah, but
the most motivated and gifted of the yeshivah-world
flocked to Brisk to hear his Talmudic lectures. It
became axiomatic throughout the Torah world that
if one wished to excel in the development of truth
— in Torah or in community activities — the
address to seek was Rav Velvel (Yiddish for Zev),
the Brisker Rav.

Known for his relentless battle against nonreligious movements, he fought with determination to undo their damage. When the Polish government passed anti-Jewish decrees, the Brisker Rav, in the company of the Chofetz Chaim, the Gerrer Rebbe and Rav Chaim Ozer Grodzinski worked feverishly toward their abolition.

In 5701/1941 he immigrated to Eretz Yisroel *via Vilna and settled in Yerushalayim. True to his style, he did not establish a formal yeshivah, but here again the elite of Torah youth crowded his beis medrash to hear his lectures. His* daas Torah *was eagerly sought, especially after the passing of the Chazon Ish. His pronouncements were respected by the masses as well as by Torah sages, who considered them the final word.*

He passed away on 9 Tishrei, 5720/1959. His sons and sons-in-law were great Torah scholars and lecturers.

uring the years 5712-13/1952-53, strong tensions prevailed in the Orthodox Jewish community throughout the world regarding the future of *Yiddishkeit* in *Eretz Yisroel*, due to the impending passage of the *"giyus banos"* (military draft for women) laws by Israel's Knesset.

Torah sages in Israel and in the Diaspora worked indefatigably to do everything possible to thwart passage of the proposed law. They unanimously concurred with the rabbinical ruling of the Chazon Ish that any form of governmental induction of women is strictly prohibited by Jewish law; and that it constitutes one of the three cardinal sins for which a Jew must be ready to die rather than transgress.

Lobbying and petitioning of all sorts were undertaken to avert the passage of the law, but to no avail. Massive demonstrations took place in New York, London and Yerushalayim with the participation of all segments of *Chareidi* Jewry, including the *Roshei Yeshivah* of all yeshivos and all Chassidic leaders. Even those who never before had taken part in any public appearances instinctively felt that this was an extraordinary situation with far-reaching repercussions affecting Jewry's future, and made their personal appearance at the demonstrations.

During those fateful days, a prominent public figure, who had been heavily involved in trying to prevent the passage of the law, visited the Brisker Rav, Harav Yitzchok Zev Soloveitchik. The *Rav* asked him whether he was continuing his efforts. His response was that since all avenues of influence were already exhausted, nothing more could be done.

The Brisker Rav's opinion, however, was different. He explained that when our Sages state: "Even when a sharp sword rests on a person's throat, he should not refrain from praying," they were referring not only to individual life-and-death crises, but also to predicaments affecting the general public. Then too, prayer is a viable option, even when everything seems lost. To better explain the concept, he related an incident that took place during the early years of his rabbinate in Brisk.

"One of the negative consequences of World War I, insofar as the Jewish population is concerned, was the proliferation of various nonreligious groups throughout Eastern Europe. A wave of leftist and Zionist parties swarmed over the continent, spreading their contaminated ideas in every community. In some cities they won a majority vote in the *kehillah* (the officially recognized governing body which set policy for all Jewish community endeavors) and dictated even purely religious matters. During one election, these groups won the leadership of the Brisk *kehillah* and took control of the Central Synagogue.

"Once, as Rosh Hashanah was approaching, I got word that the *gabboim* (administrators of synagogue rituals) organized a choir in order to 'add flavor' to the liturgy. I was opposed to this, but not on the basis of *halachah*, as I did not have the time to delve into the particulars of the case. I simply had a gut feeling that if the *gabboim* were so determined to employ a choir without consulting me, the idea must have originated in non-traditional, reform-minded circles. Due to the closeness to the holiday, I did not have time to speak to the people involved to dissuade them from going through with the choir.

"Rosh Hashanah arrived and the choir took their positions in a section of the upper gallery designated for them by the *gabboim*. Knowing that the *gabboim* would turn a deaf ear to me, I confronted the members of the choir directly, informing them that under no circumstances would I allow a choir in Brisk. I ordered them to vacate the gallery immediately.

"The members of the choir listened to me and left the platform," the *Rav* continued. "As soon as they descended, though, the *gabboim* ordered them to go up again. I followed them, ordering them again to come down. Once more they obeyed, but for a very short time; for immediately, the *gabboim* followed with their orders for them to go up and perform. The spectacle repeated itself several times: the *gabboim* instructing them to go up, while I protested, ordering them to descend.

"I thought to myself, *This entire ugly affair is starting to take the form of a Purim play. What more can I do? Haven't I tried to protest, even to stop them physically from what I consider a* חילול השם *— a desecration of G-d's holy Name? Yet, I am powerless, for the audacity of the* gabboim *has no limit.* Just as I was ready to give up, I decided to stand up to them even at the cost of exposing myself to even more ridicule and derision. I followed suit, ordering them once again to come down.

"Interestingly, this satirical spectacle ended as I strengthened my resolve. While ascending the stairs once again, the curtains in the women's gallery unexpectedly opened with screams of protest and condemnation of the *gabboim's* behavior. I was told later that, ironically, the wives of the *gabboim* were the most vocal in their protestations."

Concluding this tale, Rav Yitzchok Zev turned to his visitor to offer one more poignant dramatization of one's duty never to give up. "Let's contemplate the status of the individual for whom our Sages have instructed: 'Even when a sharp sword rests on a person's throat, he should not refrain from praying.' Imagine the following: a person was arrested on a spying charge and was incarcerated until the trial date. The authorities interrogate him using legal, and not so legal, means to extract a confession. His family hires an experienced, high-priced attorney who represents him to the best of his ability, but he is unsuccessful in swaying the judges. The prisoner is found guilty and sentenced to death.

"In desperation, the family hires an even higher-priced attorney to appeal the verdict. Yet after the legal process is over, the appeals court agrees with the original verdict.

"Let us examine for a moment this convict's likelihood of gaining freedom. Obviously, the odds are minuscule. Yet, this is exactly the scenario for which the Sages have given their instruction. As we said, the rule is not limited to individuals, but applies also to the fate of an entire nation. Prayer can turn the tables from catastrophe to unexpected resolutions of problems.

"Our task is not to allow despair to take hold in our struggle against these laws, even in the face of harsh disappointments and obvious failures. In the long haul we are bound to win."

Since that time, tens of thousands of pious young ladies have reached draft age and have not been conscripted. They have become the pride of *Klal Yisrael*, transmitting their traditional values intact to the next generation.

The Test

Harav Simcha Bunim Alter

Gerrer Rebbe

The Test

Harav Simchah Bunim Alter zt"l, the Gerrer Rebbe, author of Lev Simchah, *was born in 5658/1898. His father was known as the Imrei Emes, son of the Sfas Emes, a grandson of the founder of the Gerrer dynasty, the Chidushei HoRim. His father hired the best tutors to teach the child, in addition to his own learning sessions with him. As a young man, Simchah Bunim did everything in his power to camouflage his vast Torah knowledge, a practice he continued throughout his life. Nonetheless, people who knew him sensed that there was much more to the young man than met the eye, and that a great Torah sage was masquerading in the guise of a simple person.*

In 5687/1927 his father sent him as his emissary to Eretz Yisroel; *and after a while he was successful in establishing the now-famous Yeshivah Chidushei HoRim in Tel Aviv. His longing for his father, however, did not give him peace and in 5699/1939 he visited Poland with the clear objective of persuading his father to immigrate to* Eretz Yisrael. *During the time that his father was weighing this proposal, World War II broke out. The family was rescued from burning Warsaw through a series of miracles and immigrated to* Eretz Yisrael.

Upon the passing of the Imrei Emes in 5708/1948, Reb Simchah Bunim's oldest brother, Harav Yisrael, author of Beis Yisrael, took over the mantle of leadership as Gerrer Rebbe. Reb Simchah Bunim accepted his brother's leadership with total submission, as a dedicated Chassid. True to his personality and humility, even when approaching his golden-age years, he did whatever was feasible to hide his phenomenal Torah knowledge and tzidkus, pretending to be a simple person, earning his living in real estate.

After the passing of his brother, Reb Simchah Bunim was appointed successor. Despite his advanced age — he was then close to 80 years old — he was successful in implementing some major innovations which affected his Chassidim in many areas of day-to-day living, both on the religious front as well as in social welfare.

He is fondly remembered as a pioneer in the battle for inexpensive rental units for newly married couples; for limiting the scope of weddings and simchos; and for the extension of Chassidic communities into new cities, such as Arad, Chatzor Haglilit and Ashdod. His pleasing personality and kindheartedness won him the admiration of all segments of Chareidi Jewry in Eretz Yisrael and in the Diaspora.

He passed away on 7 Tamuz, 5752/1992. His brother, Harav Pinchas Menachem, succeeded him until his sudden passing on Shushan Purim, 5756/1996. At that time, the reigns of leadership were transferred to Reb Simchah Bunim's son.

Harav Simchah Bunim Alter was married at age 16 to his first cousin. Ten years passed until they were finally blessed with a child. One can imagine the young parents' happiness over the birth of the little baby girl, a true bundle of joy. Their happiness, however, was shortlived. Apparently, they were due for a Divine trial, testing their endurance and their absolute faith in *Hashem*: the young wife developed a severe illness, necessitating hospitalization for more than a full year.

The young man was forced to divide his daily schedule between his intensive Torah studies and keeping his wife company, offering her several hours of mental stimulation, which she so desperately needed. To be sure, people many years his senior would not prevail easily over such a series of tribulations; surely not an inexperienced young man, barely 26 years of age.

Outsiders who crossed his path in those trying days were amazed and inspired by his happy disposition, even in the face of misfortune. To his close ones, however, his behavior was no surprise at all. Although it takes a great deal of self-discipline to master absolute faith in all circumstances, this trait was the very essence of what the young man stood for: to be *Simchah* ["in a state of happiness"] Bunim. What was truly remarkable, almost unbelievable, was another dimension to the story.

With his wife's health in such a precarious condition, Rav Simchah Bunim was insistent on sparing her any additional grief. Indeed, another calamity had befallen them: their precious daughter passed away at the age of only six months, while her mother was in the hospital. The young man was intent on withholding this news from his wife, pretending the entire time that an aunt was taking care of the infant. Day after day, Rav Simchah Bunim arrived at the hospital and spent hours on end, telling his wife about the new goings-on and the milestones reached by their wonderful little girl. It took not only enormous resolve and tenacity, but also a large dose of imagination and planning, to coincide his fictitious stories of the baby's accomplishments with the normal day-by-day progression of a baby her age.

His iron will, combined with his golden heart, enabled him to do the impossible. This acid test trained him well for his future role as the leader of tens of thousands of Gerrer Chassidim, and he became one of the most beloved leaders of *Klal Yisrael.*

Deep Respect for Disciples

Harav Yechezkel Sarna

Rosh Yeshivah, Chevron Yeshivah

Deep Respect
for Disciples

Harav Yechezkel Sarna zt"l, Rosh Yeshivah *of the Chevron Yeshivah in Yerushalayim, was born in 5650/1890 in a town near Minsk, Belarus. His father, Harav Yaakov Chaim, was known as the* Maggid *[preacher] of Slonim; and his grandfather was Harav Shraga Feivel, one of the prime Torah scholars of Russia.*

In his youth, he had the z'chus to study under several of the greatest Torah sages of the generation, including Harav Zalman Sender Schapiro of Maltch, Harav Chaim Rabinowitz of Slobodka and Harav Shimon Shkop, Rosh Yeshivah of the Grodno Yeshivah. His primary rebbe, however, was the Alter *of Slobodka, Harav Nosson Notta Finkel, who displayed a special appreciation of the young man, recognizing his potential as a future leader of* Klal Yisrael.

When World War I broke out, he managed to evade conscription with the use of falsified documents. He was apprehended by the authorities, but escaped miraculously to Sislowitz. There he joined the Chofetz Chaim's yeshivah, which had set up temporary quarters. During the year and a half he spent in the company of the Chofetz Chaim he became imbued with many of the lofty traits of this outstanding tzaddik. Despite the prevailing state of anarchy and mayhem of the war, he managed to publish his first work, Toras HaOnshim.

His reputation grew and the Slobodka Rosh
Yeshivah, *Harav Moshe Mordechai Epstein, chose him*
as a suitable match for his daughter. In 5684/1924,
due to new Lithuanian draft laws, the Alter *of*
Slobodka sent him to Eretz Yisrael *as his personal*
emissary to establish a branch of the yeshivah there.
The yeshivah was established in Chevron.

The yeshivah functioned admirably for five years
until that day of infamy — the day of the Chevron
Pogrom of 5689/1929. Gathering the students who
survived the massacre, Rav Yechezkel relocated the
yeshivah to Yerushalayim. His Torah lectures, as well
as his mussar shiurim, *gained fame for their clarity*
and logic. Through the years, his classes attracted
thousands of participants, many of whom eventually
occupied rabbinical positions throughout Israel.

He passed away at the age of 80 on 6 Elul,
5729/1969. His family is known as worthy
marbitzei Torah.

On a *Motzoei Shabbos* several weeks before the passing of Harav Yechezkel Sarna, at a point when sickness had already claimed most of his strength, Rav Yechezkel mustered his failing energy to climb the steps leading to the yeshivah's main sanctuary, so that he could *daven Maariv* there.

As soon as he and his entourage stepped into the building, it immediately became apparent that the students had just finished their prayers. It was assumed that in light of the situation, the *Rosh Yeshivah* would surely return home and *daven* there. Rav Yechezkel, however, decided otherwise, insisting that they walk up the stairs to the yeshivah's main study hall. Naturally, upon hearing the news that their beloved *rebbe* was about to come to the *beis medrash*, the students waited for him with anticipation.

With slow, determined steps he climbed the stairs, finally arriving in a visibly fatigued state from the extraordinary exertion. His disciples welcomed him with respect and affection, individually greeting him with the customary *Motzoei Shabbos* greeting, "*Gut voch*," and waiting to receive a reciprocal blessing from the *Rosh Yeshivah*. He cordially pressed the hands of hundreds of students, smiling to them and exchanging some words with each one of them.

After all of the students had filed by, he *davened Maariv* and returned home in a state of total fatigue from the uncommon exertion. When he had rested awhile, his family asked him why he had put himself through such hardship. Why hadn't he simply returned home once he had missed *Maariv* in the yeshivah?

"I will explain," Rav Yechezkel said pensively. "You are looking at it simply from the *Maariv* point of view, and from that perspective you are right. I, on the other hand, had something totally different in mind. Take note of the fact that the *mitzvah* of *davening* with a *minyan* is only a rabbinical obligation, especially regarding the evening service; while performing the *mitzvah* of ואהבת לרעיך כמוך — to love a fellow Jew as oneself — is unequivocally one of the 613 primary *mitzvos*. This *mitzvah* is in a class of its own, serving in a sense, as the foundation for the entire Torah.

"As you can see, I am an elderly, sick man, and I rarely have the opportunity to fulfill this beautiful *mitzvah* in a meaningful way. I knew that my appearance at the yeshivah would evoke a feeling of mutual love and affection, something greatly surpassing the significance of *Maariv*. The great exertion was but a small price to pay for such a unique, all-encompassing *mitzvah*."

Rav Yechezkel Sarna and the Chofetz Chaim
A Story Within a Story

Those who knew Rav Yechezkel intimately assert that the year and a half he spent in the company of the Chofetz Chaim left a lifetime impact on him, greatly sensitizing him to אהבת ישראל, sincere love for every Jew. The Chofetz Chaim bestowed extraordinary attention on Rav Yechezkel and seemed to have valued his opinion greatly. One of the greatest demonstrations of this trust is related in the following story:

With the outbreak of World War I, the Russian government issued an order that all German citizens present themselves to the military authorities. At the time, there were three German students in the Chofetz Chaim's yeshivah in Radin. These lads disregarded the order, fearing that the Russian government would immediately incarcerate them as prisoners of war and they would likely be sent to central Russia or Siberia.

In the summer of 5675/1915 a visitor arrived in Radin and rented quarters adjacent to an apartment used by yeshivah students. He developed a relationship with them and in the course of time widened his circle of friends, displaying special warmth toward the German students. One day, he invited them out for a hike and upon reaching a cliff they all sat down to rest. While there, he slipped a document into the pocket of one of the students — a youth by the name of Ephraim Lebowitz. The paper was a schematic of a Russian military complex.

On the fast of the Seventeenth of Tamuz, a detail of civilian and military law-enforcement agents arrived in the middle of the night and surrounded the residence of Ephraim Lebowitz. The student was handcuffed and taken to the military penitentiary in Lida, then to Vilna, and later indicted on charges of spying and transferring military secrets to the enemy. During this time, the Chofetz Chaim expended superhuman efforts, including large sums of money, to pave the way to some common sense and objectivity, but no headway was made. The sage could not even obtain simple facts on the status and whereabouts of Ephraim.

By Divine Providence, a Jewish contractor was doing a construction job in the remote central Russian city of Panza, in the vicinity of a prison compound. Suddenly he heard someone calling to him in Yiddish, a most uncommon phenomenon in that part of Russia. He followed the sound to the prison and heard the voice of a young man identifying himself as Ephraim Lebowitz, pleading with this fellow Jew to notify the Chofetz Chaim of his whereabouts. Needless to say, the contractor initiated intensive activities on his behalf.

It was learned that his trial would take place shortly in the capital city of St. Petersburg. Despite his advanced age of close to 80, the Chofetz Chaim undertook the grueling task of traveling hundreds of kilometers to engage a prominent attorney and to appear personally at the trial. Rav Yechezkel Sarna was chosen by the Chofetz Chaim to accompany him on his fateful trip to St. Petersburg, and he consulted Rav Yechezkel throughout the ordeal.

We take the liberty to digress and relate a remarkable episode during one of these court sessions. The defense attorney called upon the Chofetz Chaim as a character witness on behalf of Ephraim. To emphasize the sage's honesty and integrity, the attorney spoke of the worldwide adulation accorded him and told the following incident to the court:

"The witness was once walking down the street and was approached by a man who asked if he could change a five-ruble bill for him. The rabbi took five singles out of his purse and handed them to the man who took the money and, without turning over the larger bill, began running. You would have expected him to run after the thief, or at the very least to scream to passersby to apprehend him. But this did not happen. Instead, the witness chased the fleeing thief, shouting: 'I forgive you! I forgive you with my whole heart! I absolve you from restitution!'"

The Chief Justice turned cynically to the attorney and asked, "Do you actually believe this story?"

"No, Your Honor, I do not," the attorney answered resolutely, to the shock of the entire courtroom.

"Then why do you relate stories that you yourself don't believe?" the judge asked with indignation.

"Tell me, Your Honor, do such stories circulate about you or me? The greatest proof of his virtue is the fact that even within his lifetime he has become a legend — with episodes like these spun around his lofty personality."

The Chofetz Chaim took the stand and testified on Ephraim's behalf. He then returned home while the case was continuing. Finally the verdict was handed down. "The criminal Ephraim Lebowitz has been found guilty as a traitor and is hereby sentenced to death. However, taking into account his young age, the sentence has been reduced to twelve years of hard labor," the Chief Justice announced.

As the aide and confidant of the Chofetz Chaim throughout the trip, Rav Yechezkel had the unpleasant task of informing the Chofetz Chaim of the outcome. Wishing to minimize his *rebbe's* pain, Rav Yechezkel took the liberty to minimize the verdict, stating that Ephraim was sentenced to six years in prison.

Hearing the terrible news, all those present burst out crying. The only one who surprisingly did not display any emotion was the Chofetz Chaim. First, he thanked *Hashem* for His kindness and mercy in sparing Ephraim's life. Then he tried to comfort everyone.

Finally, concerning the verdict, he commented drily: "They have sentenced him to six years. What utter fools they are. Are they assured of staying in power even six weeks?"

The *godol* of the generation uttered those fateful words and apparently the Heavenly court concurred. At the termination of the six-week period, on the twenty-second day of Adar, 5676/1917, Czar Nikolai of Russia was forced to abdicate the throne and all political prisoners were freed, including Ephraim Lebowitz.

The distinguished *Rosh Yeshivah* of the Kamenitz Yeshivah, Harav Boruch Ber, stated that when the story of the Chofetz Chaim's comment was told to his *rebbe*, Harav Chaim Soloveitchik, *Rav* of Brisk, he said, "The Chofetz Chaim deposed the Czar of Russia." The Brisker Rav seemed to imply that years of political unrest, including several attempted revolutions against the Czarist regime, had been unsuccessful; but when the Chofetz Chaim uttered his terse pronouncement, his propitious words tipped the Heavenly balance, and the brutal monarch was deposed. As we read in *Shiras Channah*, "He guards the steps of His devout ones, but the wicked are stilled in darkness; for not through strength does man prevail." (I *Shmuel*, 2:9)

Selfless Devotion to the Wretchedly Poor

Harav Isser Zalman Meltzer

*Rosh Yeshivah,
Yeshivah Etz Chaim*

Selfless Devotion to the Wretchedly Poor

Harav Isser Zalman Meltzer zt"l, Rosh Yeshivah of Yeshivah Etz Chaim in Yerushalayim, was born in 5630/1870 in the town of Mir, Lithuania. He received his primary education from the town's Rav, Harav Yom Tov Lipman, author of Malbushei Yom Tov. *He next traveled to Volozhin, the greatest Torah citadel in Russia and studied there for seven years under the tutelage of the illustrious Rav Chaim Soloveitchik, the future Brisker Rav. He continued to Radin to study in the yeshivah of the holy Chofetz Chaim.*

His reputation spread throughout the yeshivah world, and the widow of Rav Feivel Frank, one of the most prominent Torah sages and wealthiest Jews in Lithuania, chose him as the right match for her talented daughter. They settled in Kovno along with their brother-in-law, Harav Moshe Mordechai Epstein, future Rosh Yeshivah *of the Slobodka Yeshivah. Rav Isser Zalman befriended many Torah sages there, especially the world-renown Rav of Kovno, Harav Yitzchok Elchonon Spector.*

In 5654/1894 he and his brother-in-law were appointed to serve as lecturers in the Slobodka Yeshivah. Three years later, the Alter *of Slobodka, Harav Nosson Notta Finkel, designated him to establish a yeshivah in Slutzk. Under his leadership, the yeshivah thrived, eventually enrolling hundreds of students.*

Following the immigration of the Radbaz, who served as Rav *of Slutzk, to* Eretz Yisrael, *Rav Isser Zalman was elected to succeed him in 5663/1903. He took on this task in addition to his responsibilities as* Rosh Yeshivah. *A number of years later, after the Communist Revolution, the Communist grip became intolerable and the yeshivah moved across the border to Kletzk, Poland. In 5685/1925 Rav Isser Zalman went to* Eretz Yisrael *and assumed the position of* Rosh Yeshivah *of the Etz Chaim Yeshivah of Yerushalayim. He appointed his son-in-law, Harav Aaron Kotler of later Lakewood fame, to succeed him as* Rosh Yeshivah *of the yeshivah in Kletzk.*

In Eretz Yisrael, *Rav Isser Zalman was very active both in disseminating Torah and in communal affairs. He was considered the elder Torah sage of the Holy Land and was consulted on all matters affecting* Klal Yisrael. *He was involved in all the struggles of* Chareidi *Jewry in maintaining their Torah lifestyle, especially regarding the exemption of yeshivah students from army service. His kindheartedness and devotion to others were legendary, winning him admirers throughout all segments of Jewry.*

Rav Isser Zalman served as Rosh Yeshivah *of major* yeshivos *for over six decades and had the pleasure of seeing third- and fourth-generation Torah scholars arise from among his disciples. His classic work, the seven-volume* Even HoOzel *on the* Rambam, *won international acclaim.*

He passed away on 6 Kislev, 5714/1954, leaving a generation of great Torah scholars and Roshei Yeshivah *in* Eretz Yisrael *and America.*

At the outbreak of World War I in the summer of 1914, many of the Jews living near the war front in Poland escaped across the border to Slutzk, Russia. Living conditions were atrocious; most refugees were quartered in the local synagogues, lacking even basic necessities. Though life was somehow tolerable during the summer months, when winter arrived the situation became critical, with almost no fuel or clothing available.

The Slutzker Rav, Harav Isser Zalman Meltzer, took personal charge of the situation, carrying the entire financial responsibility for the refugees. In addition, his house was open at all hours of the day and night to allow those in need to find a receptive ear to their woes.

The war impacted deeply not only on the refugees, but also on the entire Jewish community. When community leaders got word that their *Rav's* household was in a dismal state of affairs — that his salary did not suffice for even one quarter of his budget — they scheduled a special meeting to discuss the matter.

The *shammos* got wind of the committee's special session, and hurried to notify the *Rav* that in the near future his financial situation hopefully would improve. The *Rav* made a note of the time and place of the meeting and thanked the *shammos* for bringing him the good tidings.

When the day came, the *Rav* was there to join the meeting. The president opened the session with brief remarks, pointing out the dire circumstances of their beloved *Rav* and recommending that a substantial increase in his salary be approved. Immediately after, the *Rav* was given the opportunity to comment.

"Dear committee members, leadership of the Slutzk Jewish community," he began. "First, let me take this opportunity to thank you for having me and my family in mind. I have but one small plea and I respectfully request a unanimous vote on it. My request is to kindly remove the subject of my salary from the agenda.

"All of you, dear gentlemen, are familiar with the terrible conditions of the refugees who are living in squalor. They are exposed to hunger and need. Especially now during the bitter winter months, they lack even the most basic of human needs such as warm clothing and blankets. In no way do I underestimate your kind attention and contribution to our unfortunate brothers and sisters. My request is simple: the money you would have earmarked toward my salary should be given to them instead."

There was a brief debate among the committee members and a consensus was reached that both items were of equal importance. They would provide for both the *Rav's* needs and those of the refugees. The *Rav*, however, was adamant.

"Pardon me for being so forceful, but I do ask each and every committee member to do me this small favor: remove the salary increase from the agenda," the *Rav* literally begged. "Thank G-d, I have sufficient funds for my family's needs. Should my salary be increased even incrementally, it would automatically reduce the amount allocated to the poor."

With no alternative, the committee reluctantly acquiesced, and the entire session was devoted to the refugees' plight, with some important decisions reached to aid them significantly.

It is worthwhile to take a brief glimpse at Rav Isser Zalman's true financial picture when saying, "Thank G-d, I have sufficient funds for my family's needs." As mentioned above, his salary did not come close to meeting his needs, and his *Rebbetzin* helped supplement their income.

Throughout most of the night she baked rolls in her primitive oven, selling them in the morning to women who had access to the military personnel who could afford to buy fresh rolls. In addition, the *Rav* and the *Rebbetzin* rented out one room of their small apartment, with their entire family crowding into the little space left, so that an additional few rubles could be earned. Even with these "riches," the family could not meet their barest minimum needs. Yet an increase in salary was out of the question, if it was at the expense of Jewish war refugees.

Rav Isser Zalman finally agreed to a salary increase the following summer, only after the authorities had relocated most of the refugees.

The Essence of Honesty

Harav Shmuel Ehrenfeld
Rav of Mattersdorf

The Essence
of Honesty

Harav Shmuel Ehrenfeld zt"l, Rav of Mattersdorf was born in 5651/1891. His father was Harav Simchah Bunim, son of the Chasan Sofer, who was a grandson of the Chasam Sofer. He grew up in an atmosphere permeated with the holiness of this pillar of Hungarian Jewry. While still a teenager, he received his rabbinical ordination from the greatest Torah sages of the era, including Harav Yosef Engel and Harav Meir Arik of Turna. He also visited the Chassidic leaders of Galicia, especially the illustrious Belzer Rebbe, Harav Yissochor Ber Rokeach.

In 5686/1926 his father passed away and Rav Shmuel was elected to succeed him. He prevailed over the pressures of being the Rav of a community the size and caliber of Mattersdorf, and was not deterred from placing his strongest efforts in the yeshivah, directing it with exemplary wisdom and dedication.

With the Nazi invasion of Austria after the infamous Anschluss, the earth began to burn under the feet of the tens of thousands of Jews suddenly caught under Nazi tyranny. Rav Shmuel attempted to mitigate some of the harsh decrees, but avenues of action were limited.

After many trials and tribulations, he immigrated to the United States in 5698/1938. Within one month of his arrival, he had already founded Yeshivah Ch'san Sofer, which eventually grew to become one of the largest Torah centers in Brooklyn. He was also active in many communal affairs and the strengthening of Torah in all phases of life, with special interests in Sabbath observance and family purity.

In 5719/1959 he visited Eretz Yisrael *and planted the seeds of one of the primary* Chareidi *neighborhoods in Yerushalayim. His efforts eventually bore beautiful fruit, in the form of Kiryat Mattersdorf.*

He passed away on the second day of Shavuos, 5740/1980. His children and grandchildren carry the torch he lit, illuminating America and Israel with Torah.

While still a young man, Harav Simchah Bunim Ehrenfeld once returned home and came upon a most bizarre scene. His father, Harav Shmuel Ehrenfeld, was busy taking out *seforim* from the bookcase one by one. He looked at the inside of the front cover of each *sefer,* and then returned it to its place. He went through a whole row of *seforim* repeating this procedure. Occasionally, however, after peeking into the front cover, he put the *sefer* aside. Upon completing the entire bookcase, he continued on to the next bookcase.

To his son, it was indeed a most puzzling spectacle. To be sure, he had watched his father on countless occasions removing a series of *seforim* when preparing for a lecture or public address. But at those times he easily identified the *sefer* he wished to use by its title on the outside cover. Occasionally he looked inside the *sefer* in order to identify it further; in rare cases he even opened it to the table of contents. But this time, the procedure was totally different. He did not so much as glance at any information whatsoever. Noticing his son's quizzical look, the father explained what he was trying to do.

"As you know, shortly we will be hosting a very distinguished visitor, Harav Shmuel Avrohom Zeltenreich, the *Rav* of Tchakave, who will be coming to meet you as a possible *shidduch* for his daughter. It is customary for Torah sages to browse through the bookcases, seeking out new *seforim* they might not have seen yet, or very old ones, which are not commonly available.

"It is very likely that our guest will do just that. He will probably note the contents of the various bookcases in our house, and no doubt will be quite impressed with the large quantity of *seforim* we possess.

"Truthfully, however, not all the *seforim* are mine. Some belong to you; you received them at your Bar Mitzvah or acquired them over the years. Had I left the *seforim* in their place, I would be giving the Tchakever Rav a false impression about the size of my personal library. Our Sages have taught that a subdivision of the prohibition against theft is גניבת דעת, [literally, 'stealing of the mind'] which is meant to prohibit any form of misrepresentation. I have therefore removed each *sefer* bearing your name on the inside front cover, so that the remaining ones are actually mine."

Epilogue:

The Tchakever Rav was obviously impressed with the young man and the *shidduch* was arranged to the satisfaction of both parties. The young man is today's Mattersdorfer Rav, who succeeded his illustrious father in his rabbinical position.

Eliyahu, the Guardian of Bris Milah

Harav Chaim Zanvil Abramowitz

Ribnitzer Rebbe

Eliyahu, the Guardian of Bris Milah

Harav Chaim Zanvil Abramowitz zt"l, the Ribnitzer
Rebbe, was born in the town of Boteshan, Romania in
5656/1896. He lost his father when he was only 3
years old. His mother took him to the Shtefenesht
Rebbe, Harav Avrohom Matisyahu, who reared him
as if he were his own child. In one of his letters, the
Ribnitzer Rebbe writes regarding his foster father, "he
personally taught me from aleph-beis *through Osios*
d'Rabbi Akiva" (a complex work of Kabbalah). In this
noble household, young Chaim Zanvil was able to
develop to his full spiritual capacity in Torah as well
as his quest for superior levels of kedushah.

The Shtefenesht Rebbe sent him to study in
Kishinev in the yeshivah of Harav Yehuda Leib
Zierelson, one of the noted Torah sages of the
generation. The elderly rabbi exhibited special
affection for the youngster and treated him with rare
respect. Prior to his departure from Kishinev, he
earned rabbinical ordination from Rav Zierelson.
The certificate of ordination itself bespeaks the
young Rav's erudition with the following unusual
accolade: "...He is adept even in the innermost
facets of Torah, like one of the sages of yesteryear."

During the Holocaust Reb Chaim Zanvil was
exiled to Transnistria, a desolate region under the rule

of German and Romanian Nazis. The majority of Jews there perished from hunger and disease as well as from cold-blooded murder. During this dreadful period, the Rebbe's noble character surfaced in its finest form. He served as shochet, chazzan and mohel — but above all, as an angel of mercy to whom everyone turned for soothing and comfort.

After the liberation, he settled in Ribnitz, a town near Chernowitz, Moldavia. To his dismay, that region fell under Communist rule with its relentless oppression of religion. Many kehillah functionaries were sentenced to prison terms; others were banished to Siberia.

Reb Chaim Zanvil, however, was not ready to relinquish even one of his communal activities. Together with a select group of dedicated Lubavitch activists, he organized prayer groups and Torah sessions, constructed a mikvah and engaged in shechitah. He clandestinely performed bris milah on hundreds of Jewish children. In 5732/1972, he finally immigrated to Israel and after one year there, moved to America.

His mesiras nefesh in pursuit of mitzvos was legendary. His love for his Creator was overwhelming: no obstacle stood in his way and no danger intimidated him from serving Hashem in every way he could. Throughout his life he frequently fasted, spending his days in prayer and Torah study. At midnight, he bemoaned churban Beis HaMikdash with his hours-long Tikkun Chatzos. He was known as a singularly holy person whose prayers and blessings had an impact in Heaven.

He passed away at close to 100 on the 24th day of Tishrei, 5756/1995. The Ribnitzer Rebbe did not leave children, but the hundreds of Chaim Zanvils named after him have memorialized him for eternity.

T hroughout his entire life, the Ribnitzer Rebbe, Harav Chaim Zanvil Abramowitz, dedicated himself to the mitzvah of circumcision — initiating Jewish boys into the Covenant of Abraham. No hardship stood in his way, not even the long hand of the N.K.V.D., the brutal Russian secret police. The Rebbe traveled from one Soviet republic to another and from town to hamlet in pursuit of this cardinal mitzvah.

Once, during World War II, he was invited by the wife of a high-ranking Russian Jewish officer to circumcise her son. Her husband, a passionate Communist, was vociferously opposed to this "outmoded superstitious practice." Despite his wife's pleading not to disconnect their last tie to their people, the man remained adamant in his refusal to allow the bris. Providentially, the officer received a call from military headquarters to report immediately to his base. His wife capitalized on the situation and summoned Reb Chaim Zanvil to hurry and perform the bris, lest her husband show up unexpectedly.

During that period of time, the Ribnitzer Rebbe often included the legendary Chabad emissary, Harav Mendel Futerfass, in many of his vital activities. Together, they embarked on their journey to the lady's home, outfitted with all necessary bris paraphernalia and medical first-aid equipment. Upon arrival, the lady directed them to a shack at the back of her house, so that their activity could be better hidden. They shuttered the windows and the Rebbe performed the bris.

To their horror, something out of the ordinary took place. The baby was bleeding incessantly and nothing the Rebbe or Reb Mendel did could make the bleeding stop. Gradually, the child's face paled and it seemed as if the end was approaching.

The mother stood at the child's bedside, sobbing bitterly. As the situation became more desperate, she vented her frustration and anger squarely at them, berating them for their "primitive methods." Reb Chaim Zanvil and Reb Mendel were fully cognizant of the far-reaching repercussions should their mission end in tragedy. They would obviously be arrested on a series of charges including manslaughter, practicing medicine without proper schooling and appropriate licensing, in addition to the serious crime of practicing Jewish religious rites — a felony which was punishable with banishment to Siberia's Gulags.

Far worse, they feared, the story would surely make headlines throughout Russia, creating a massive *chilul Hashem*. Under duress, the mother would surely point an accusing finger at them for allegedly coercing her to allow a "cruel, inhumane ritual of circumcision."

Regarding those tense moments, Reb Mendel relates: "I gazed into Reb Chaim Zanvil's face which was glowing with a heavenly gleam unlike anything I had ever witnessed before. His head was bent slightly backwards, as if he were speaking directly toward the heavens with an intense prayer to the One Above to save the child, if for no other reason than to prevent a grave *chilul Hashem*.

"Then I witnessed an open miracle," Reb Mendel continued with animation. "Suddenly the child awakened and abruptly, without any additional medication, the blood stopped flowing. It was as close as anyone could get to *techiyas hameisim* — the revival of the deceased.

" 'Is the Rebbe performing visible miracles?' I asked. The Rebbe's humble response was, 'Eliyahu, the guardian of every *bris milah*, is standing alongside us, as he does at every *bris*. Isn't the healing of this child also in his domain?'"

An Inspiring Precedent

Harav Moshe Yitzchak Gewirtzman, Pshevorsker Rebbe of Antwerp — fondly known as Reb Itzik'l — often related the following story about the Divrei Chaim, the venerated Sanzer Rav, at the traditional gathering on the eve of a *bris* known as *vach nacht*:

On the 28th day of Iyar, 5624/1874 a baby boy was born to the daughter of Reb Moshe Zishes, one of the most distinguished townspeople of Sanz. (Appropriately, his gravesite is adjacent to that of the Sanzer Rav.) As scheduled, the *bris* took place on the eighth day from birth, the first day of Shavuos. In addition to serving as *sandek*, the Divrei Chaim also performed the *bris*.

Uncharacteristically, he did not ask the child's father, Reb Moshe Leib Schlussel, to name the child, but exclaimed "*veyikorei shmo b'Yisrael Dovid* — he shall be named in Israel [as a member of the Jewish nation] — Dovid," apparently naming him for *Dovid HaMelech* whose *yahrzeit* falls on the first day of Shavuos.

The happy parents took the child home. After several hours had passed, the baby suddenly began bleeding profusely. The parents tried every home remedy, to no avail. They fetched a doctor who tried various techniques, but finally gave up in frustration. Reluctantly, he notified the parents that they should shortly expect the inevitable.

The child's mother immediately rushed to the synagogue where the Divrei Chaim was conducting his *tish*. In the women's gallery, the young mother raised her voice in a bitter cry. Hearing her anguished wails, the Divrei Chaim inquired what had happened. He was told that Reb Moshe Zishes' daughter was crying over the fate of her just-circumcised son Dovid who was bleeding beyond control.

Notwithstanding the large crowd at the *tish*, which included dozens of notable rabbis from throughout Galicia and Hungary, the Rebbe summoned her to come to him. She informed him that the physician had already given up hope for the child. The Rebbe requested that she leave her *sterntichel* (a costly gold-embroidered headband) to serve as collateral for a *pidyon*. (When visiting a Rebbe with a request, Chassidim leave a donation called a *pidyon*.) He then instructed her to return home and bathe the baby in hot water. He blessed the baby, wishing him a speedy recovery. Once again, he stressed to the mother that she should totally disregard the doctor's prognosis.

The mother rushed home and prepared the bath for the baby. When the midwife became aware that the infant was about to be put into hot water she ardently protested that heat tends to exacerbate the bleeding rather than staunch it. The mother, however, ignored her protestations, placing her faith in the venerated Divrei Chaim and following his directives. Upon submerging the child in the tub, the bleeding ceased immediately and the child totally recuperated.

After Shavuos, the Rebbe sent a message to her, telling her to redeem her *sterntichel* for five rubles, which would be allocated for charity. He then said, "Your son will, with the help of *Hashem*, grow up to be a great Torah sage and will merit longevity."

The Divrei Chaim's *brachah* came true in its entirety. Rav Dovid Schlussel authored eight major works on an array of Torah topics. He was eventually appointed as *Rosh Beis Din* — Chief Rabbinical Judge — of the city of Munkacs and was recognized as one of the stellar Torah authorities of Eastern Europe.

He passed away at 76. Several months later, his youngest daughter gave birth to a baby boy who was named after him: Dovid — who is the author of this book.

The Wisdom of
Gentle Persuassion

Harav
Shlomo
Halberstam

Bobover Rav

The Wisdom of Gentle Persuassion

*Harav Shlomo Halberstam zt"l, the Bobover Rav,
was born in 5668/1908. His father was Harav Ben
Zion, son of Harav Shlomo, founder of the Bobov
dynasty and grandson of the illustrious Divrei
Chaim of Sanz. Young Shlomo's outstanding mental
capacity in conjunction with his diligence in Torah
created the perfect combination for his future role
as one of the builders of Yiddishkeit after the
Holocaust. He was ordained by some of the greatest
Torah sages of Galicia; and, before reaching the age
of 30, he served as Rav in Bobov, filling in for his
father who had relocated to Tchebin for a five-year
period. Those years served as a testing ground for
his future leadership positions: he succeeded in
challenging undertakings, all accomplished in a
most pleasant, peaceful and amiable fashion.*

*At the outbreak of World War II, he and his
father escaped to Lemberg. On the fourth of Av
5701/1941 his father was killed, הי"ד, and Rav
Shlomo escaped to the Bochnia Ghetto. The
situation there was desperate, with death and
disease rampant. In Bochnia, the Rav lost his
Rebbetzin and two children. He managed to
escape with his only surviving child, Naftali, to
Budapest, and then to Bucharest. Despite the*

turmoil and extreme danger, he was actively involved in the rescue of many Jews, often at the risk of his own life.

Immediately after the liberation, he settled in Bari, Italy, where he took care of many war orphans. Working feverishly on an array of religious and social projects, he rebuilt the shattered lives of war survivors. After a brief sojourn in London, he finally arrived at the shores of the United States in 5706/1946.

For over half a century he was successful establishing generations of Torah-true Chassidim in America. His all-encompassing kehillah was exemplary, as was his comprehensive educational network, with an enrollment of thousands of students.

Branches of Bobov have opened in many Chareidi population centers. The Rav also established his own shtetl in Eretz Yisrael, in the town of Bat Yam. Its first-rate yeshivah draws students from around the world.

The Bobover Rav was distinct in his strong emphasis on shalom — peace. Throughout his life he stood firm, preventing any semblance of confrontation, always ready to forfeit his own honor and status for the higher goal of harmony. Indeed, he was most successful in imbuing his entire community with this outstanding trait — a true kiddush Hashem, a sanctification of Hashem's Name.

He returned his soul to his Creator on Rosh Chodesh Av, 5760/2000, the yahrzeit of Aaron HaKohen, the great promoter of shalom. His son succeeded him as leader of the Bobov community.

man once came to the Bobover Rav, Harav Shlomo Halberstam, regarding a sticky financial problem. This person (we will call him Reuven) was a remodeler who had contracted to install an ultramodern kitchen with the newest appliances for a customer (we will call him Shimon) for a large sum of money. The contract called for installment payments throughout the job and the customer had kept to the deal. Immediately after completion, however, with an outstanding balance of several thousand dollars, he refused to honor his commitment.

Weeks and months passed and the amount was not paid. Reuven tried whatever means possible to collect, calling him daily and demanding some form of payment schedule, but to no avail. Because Shimon was a Bobover Chassid, Reuven came to the Rav requesting his assistance.

The Rav listened attentively to all the details and asked some questions. He wanted to know the specifics about the raw materials used, their country of origin and similar particulars. Despite his absolute befuddlement at the Rav's interest in the technical details, Reuven answered all questions.

Shortly after Reuven left, the Rav asked his assistant to get in touch with Shimon and to invite him to visit. Hearing that the Rav wished to see him, he left in middle of work and came over immediately. The Rav welcomed Shimon with his characteristically sparkling smile and reassuring warmth, inviting him to sit down next to him, while he made conversation about the welfare of Shimon's family, their health and education. After a few minutes, the Rav addressed him in an intimate, whispering tone, saying: "Shimon, my dear, I have invited you here in order to get your opinion on a specific subject. You know me in the capacity of Rav, a spiritual leader. But I have another role to play, and that is to be a good husband to my *Rebbetzin*.

"Recently, it occurred to me that our kitchen is quite old and neglected, and I've heard that you have recently installed a beautiful new kitchen; I was wondering if you would mind sharing your experiences with me." The Rav led him to the kitchen and pointed out his general plan, surprising Shimon immensely with his familiarity with the technical details of kitchen remodeling.

"My main concern," the Rav explained, "is whether you and your wife were totally satisfied with the workmanship, and if the work met your original specifications. If so, it might be worthwhile for the *Rebbetzin* to visit your home and see for herself."

"It will be an absolute delight and honor to host the *Rebbetzin* in our home," Shimon said enthusiastically. "The kitchen is, *boruch Hashem*, totally finished and my wife and I are exceptionally happy with it. I am certain that the *Rebbetzin* will also be pleased with it," Shimon said with delight.

"One more little question to you, Shimon," the Rav said. "There is something that concerns me more than anything else. I've been told that often a contractor will do excellent work, but at the conclusion of the job there are dozens of loose ends: though they are minor, these unfinished details are very irksome to the housewife who is eager to see the job totally finished. I was wondering, how was your experience regarding this concern?"

"I'll be totally forthright with the Rav," Shimon said. "My wife and I were both absolutely satisfied, both with the workmanship as well as with the final touches. Our contractor did not leave a single item unfinished."

Hearing this truly enthusiastic report about the contractor, the Rav again asked Shimon to join him in his study and personally offered him a chair. He then asked the *gabbai* to kindly bring in some *kibud* (light refreshments) "for our dear visitor." Shimon was overwhelmed, not knowing how to handle so much attention, first as the Rav's personal consultant, and then as the Rav's "dear visitor."

After tasting some of the *kibud*, the Rav turned to Shimon and began talking to him in a loving, fatherly tone. "Shimon, my dear. I have an important request to ask of you. I have now heard from your own mouth the details about your new kitchen and how totally satisfied both you and your wife are with all facets of the job. I wish to share with you a statement from our Sages. *Chazal* teach us that a man's personality can be identified "*b'kiso, b'koso ub'kaaso*"— with his purse [money], with his cup [when intoxicated] and when he's angry. Note that money is one of the key elements in determining the values of a human being.

"Let me give you some insight into the phenomenal significance of this statement. *Hashem's* relationship with man is reciprocal. If a person deals with others with integrity, then *Hashem* showers that person with abundance and prosperity. On the other hand, if we shortchange others, then *Hashem* will do likewise and will put us at the same disadvantage, a prospect we hope will never come to pass. I ask you, Shimon, my dear, do yourself a favor and pay the bill you owe Reuven expeditiously."

The Rav's words, spoken with kindness and love and without the slightest trace of accusation, had the proper effect. That very afternoon Shimon paid the bill in full to the satisfaction of his friend Reuven, to the satisfaction of his beloved Rav and to the satisfaction of his Father in Heaven — *HaKadosh Boruch Hu.*

Glossary

Aaron HaKohen — Biblical Aaron, brother of Moses

Adar — name of a month on the Jewish calendar

agunos — plural of *agunah*, a woman whose husband's whereabouts are unknown; thus she is prohibited to remarry until resolution of her marital status

ahavas Hashem — love of G-d

aleph-beis — Hebrew alphabet

Alter — elder; spiritual head of a yeshivah

Ari HaKadosh — one of the most prominent Kabbalists of all time

Av — name of a month on the Jewish calendar

avodas Hashem — service of G-d

beis medrash — study hall; synagogue; main sanctuary of a yeshivah

Beis Yosef — author of *Shulchan Aruch* [Code of Jewish Law]; prominent commentary on the *Tur*

Beis HaMikdash — Holy Temple in Jerusalem

ben Torah, (pl.) bnai Torah — a person dedicated to living his life according to the Torah

bitachon — trust in G-d

bitul Torah — the prohibition against losing time from Torah study

blinder — blind man (Yiddish)

bachur — unmarried young man

baruch Hashem — Thank G-d

braissa — addendum to the Mishnah

bris, bris milah — circumcision (also known as the Covenant of Abraham)

brachah — a blessing

brachah v'hatzlachah — blessing and success

C

Chabad — Chassidic group founded in the 18th century

chadorim — plural of *cheder* (see below)

challos — plural of *challoh*, festive bread eaten on Sabbath and holidays

Chareidi — Orthodox

Chassid, (pl.) Chassidim — a member of one of many groups ascribing to the philosophy and lifestyle of *chassidus* (see below)

Chassidus — a religious movement founded in the 18th century that stresses deep introspection; acceptance of the leadership of a Rebbe in all phases of life; and cheerful positive thinking

Chazal — Talmudic sages

chazzan — cantor

cheder, (pl.) chadorim — elementary Torah school

chesed — benevolence; good deed

Cheshvan — name of a month on the Jewish calendar

chidushei Torah (pl.) — original Torah thoughts expressed in writing or orally

chilul Hashem — desecration of the Name (of G-d)

chol hamoed — intermediate days between the first and last days of the holidays of Passover and Succos

chosson — bridegroom

Chumash/Rashi — Five Books of Moses with Rashi's commentary (see *Rashi* below)

chupah — canopy; formal marriage ceremony

churban — destruction; sometimes denotes Holocaust

churban Beis HaMikdash — destruction of the Holy Temples in Jerusalem

chutzpah — brazenness; gall

D

daas Torah — Torah ruling; a determination made by Torah sages

daven — pray

davening — prayer service

dayan, (pl.) dayanim — rabbinical judge(s)

Dovid HaMelech — King David

dvar Torah — a Torah thought expressed orally or in writing

E

Eida HaChareidis — independent rabbinate in Jerusalem

Elul — name of a month on the Jewish calendar

emes —truth

emunah — absolute faith in G-d

emunas chachomim — faith in the judgment of sages

Eretz Yisrael — the land of Israel

erev — the day before Sabbath or holidays

G

gabbai, (pl.) gabboim — administrator(s) of synagogue rituals

Gan Eden — afterlife; Paradise

gaon — genius; Torah sage

gedolei hador — greatest Torah sages of the generation

gedolei Yisrael — Torah sages

Gehinom — afterlife; Hell

Gemora — Talmud

giyus banos — conscription of women into the armed services *godol* — an extraordinary Torah sage

godol b'Yisrael — see *godol*, literally a sage in the nation of Israel

godol hador — the greatest Torah sage of the generation

Gut voch — "Good week"; salutation at the close of Sabbath as the new week begins

H

hachnossas kallah — fund for wedding expenses of needy brides

hachnossas orchim — [the *mitzvah* of] welcoming guests to one's home

hadran — customary prayer at the conclusion [*siyum*] of a tractate of the Talmud

HaKodosh Baruch Hu — G-d

hakoras hatov — expressing gratitude for a service or a good deed rendered

halachah — code of Jewish law (halachic: pertaining to Jewish law or in accordance with it)

Hallel — praise; special prayer of praise to G-d recited on holidays

Hashem — G-d

hashgachah pratis — Divine Providence; G-d's interest and influence even on trivial matters

hatzlachah — success

hesped, (pl.) hespedim — eulogy, eulogies

I

illuy — genius; prodigy

Im yirtzeh Hashem — G-d willing

Iyar — name of month on the Jewish calendar

K *Kabbalah* — mysticism; branch of Jewish thought dealing with the mystical aspects of Torah

Kaddish — special prayer recited to honor the deceased

kallah — bride

kashrus — observance of Jewish dietary laws

Kaylim — food vessels; tractate in Talmud (Mishnah only) dealing with the laws of vessels

kedoshim utehorim — the holy and the pure

Kedushah — holiness; spirituality

kedushas haShabbos — sanctity of the Sabbath

kedushas Yisroel — sanctity of the Jewish nation; observance of the laws of family purity

kehillah — Jewish community; congregation

kibud — light refreshment

kibud ame — respecting one's mother

Kiddush — prayer of sanctification recited over a cup of wine on the Sabbath and holidays

kiddush Hashem — sanctification of His (G-d's) Name

Kiddush Shem Shomayim — sanctification of the Name of Heaven (G-d's Name)

Kislev — name of a Jewish month on the Jewish calendar

Klal Yisrael — the Jewish nation

Koheles — Book of Ecclesiastes

kollel — Talmudic institute for married men

Kotel HaMaaravi — the Western Wall in Jerusalem

L *l'chaim* — literally "to life"; raising a cup of wine or whiskey and wishing one another good fortune

lechem mishnah — "two loaves of bread" required at each of the Sabbath meals

LeDovid Mizmor — name of a psalm, "To David, a Hymn"

limud haTorah — Torah study

lishmah — for the exclusive objective of doing G-d's will

Maariv — evening prayer

Maggid — orator

marbitzei Torah — disseminators of Torah; Torah educators

Mashgiach, Mashgiach Ruchani, (pl.) Mashgichim — spiritual director of a yeshivah

mitzvah, (pl.) mitzvos — a Torah commandment; a good deed

Melaveh Malkah — celebratory meal eaten at the culmination of the Sabbath

mesiras nefesh — self-sacrifice

mesivta — post elementary yeshivah

mikvah, (pl.) mikvaos — ritual bath(s)

Minchah — afternoon prayer

minhagei Yisrael — Jewish customs

minyan — quorum of ten Jewish males gathered for prayer

Mishnah — the basis of the Talmud elucidated in more detail in the Gemora

mohel — circumciser; person who performs *bris milah*

Moshe Rabbeinu — Moses our Teacher

Motzoei Shabbos — Saturday evening following the Sabbath

Moshiach Tzidkeinu — the Holy Messiah

mussar — Jewish ethics and philosophy

 na'anooim — the ritual shaking of the Four Species (lulav, esrog, etc.)

nachas — pleasure; satisfaction

Ne'ilah — the final prayer recited on Yom Kippur

neshimoh — breath; inhalation

neshomah — soul

nigun — tune; melody

nisoyon — a challenge

Nissan — name of a month on the Jewish calendar

nistar — secretive; a great person in the guise of simplicity

P

parshas (Vayigash) — weekly Torah portion (of *Vayigash*)

pasuk — verse in Torah or Bible

payos — sidelocks

pidyon — money accompanying a request to a Rebbe

pidyon shvuyim — the release of prisoners, usually through ransom

pikuach nefesh — a life-or-death danger

Pirkei Avos — Ethics of our Fathers, the Talmudic tractate dealing with ethics

R

rabbonim — rabbis

rasha — wicked person

Rashi — one of the greatest early commentators on Bible and the Talmud

Rav — Rabbi (title)

rebbe — religious educator

Rebbe (Rebbe of____) — Chassidic leader

Rebbetzin — wife of a rabbi

rodeph — pursuer

Rosh Beis Din — Chief rabbinical justice

Rosh Chaburah — leader of a specific religious group

Rosh Yeshivah, (pl.) Roshei Yeshivah — Dean(s) of yeshivah(s) (title)

S

sandek — one who holds the infant during a circumcision (accorded as an honor)

sefer, (pl.) seforim — Jewish religious book(s)

Selichos — series of prayers of atonement in preparation for the High Holidays *semichah* — rabbinical ordination

Shabbos — Sabbath

Shabbos HaMalkah — the Sabbath Queen

Shacharis — morning prayer

Shalom aleichem — customary greeting in Hebrew

shalom bayis — matrimonial harmony

shammos — one responsible for the care and upkeep of a synagogue

Shas — Talmud

shechitah — slaughtering of animals in accordance with Jewish law

sherut leumi — government-controlled public service for women in Israel

shev shmaatesa — intricate commentary on *Choshen Mishpat* [the volume of the Code of Jewish Law dealing with monetary matters]

Shevat — name of a month on the Jewish calendar

shidduch — matrimonial match

shikun — building project; township

Shiras Channah — "Channah's Song," expressing gratitude to G-d for granting her a son

shiur, (pl.) shiurim — lecture(s); lesson(s)

shiurei Torah — lessons or lectures on a Torah subject

Shlomo HaMelech — King Solomon

Shmuel — Book of Samuel

shochet, (pl.) shochtim — one who slaughters animals in accordance with Jewish law

shtetl — a small town; small Jewish town in Eastern Europe

shtreimel — a round fur hat worn by some Chassidic groups on Sabbath and holidays

shul — synagogue

Shulchan Aruch — Code of Jewish Law

Shviis — name of a tractate in Talmud

simchah, (pl.) simchos — happiness; a festivity, such as a Bar Mitzvah or a wedding

Sivan — name of a month on the Jewish calendar

siyata d'Shmaya — Providential aid from G-d

siyum — completion; ceremony marking the completion of the study of a tractate of Talmud

Siyum HaShas — [ceremony marking] the completion of the study of the entire Talmud

sofer — a ritual scribe

sterntichel — an elaborate headband

sugyos haShas — major Talmudic subjects

T

tallis — prayer shawl

talmid chacham — Torah sage

Talmud Bavli, Yerushalmi — the Talmud(s) composed in Babylonia and Jerusalem respectively

Tamuz — name of a month on the Jewish calendar

techiyas hameisim — revival of the deceased

tefillin — phylacteries, used during prayer

Tehillim — Book of Psalms

Teveria — city of Tiberias

Teves — name of a month on the Jewish calendar

Tikkun Chatzos — midnight prayer commemorating the destruction of the Holy Temple

tikkunim — literally mending; elevating the spiritual status of oneself or others in a structured, organized fashion

tish — Chassidic "table" (meal) conducted by a Rebbe

Tishrei — name of a month on the Jewish calendar

Torah lishmah — studying Torah for the sake of pleasing G-d, without the least ulterior motive

Tosfos — a major commentary on Talmud

treif — nonkosher

Tur — an early compilation of the entire Code of Jewish Law

tzaddik, (pl.) tzaddikim — highly righteous person (s)

Tzfas — city of Safed
tzidkus — holiness, righteousness
tznius — modesty

V

vach nacht — festivity on the eve before a *bris*
Viduy — the customary confession for those on the threshold of death

Y

Yad HaChazakah — Rambam's Code of Jewish Law
yahrzeit — annual commemoration for the deceased on the Hebrew date of death
Yerushalayim — city of Jerusalem
yeshivah, (pl.) yeshivos — Jewish religious school(s); rabbinical seminary(ies)
yetzer hara — evil inclination, often personified
Yid — Jew
Yiddishe shtetl — Jewish town (emulating small Jewish towns of Eastern Europe)
Yiddishkeit — Judaism; an all-encompassing Torah lifestyle
yiras Hashem — awe; fear of G-d
yiras Shomayim — awe; fear of G-d (lit. fear of Heavenly Power)
Yoma — tractate in the Talmud dealing with Yom Kippur
Yom Tov — holiday
Yosef HaTzaddik — Biblical Joseph, known for his righteousness

Z

Zaidy — grandfather
z'chus, (pl.) z'chuyos — honor, privilege(s)
z'miros — melodies; songs sung during Sabbath and holiday meals
zocheh — to merit; be privileged
zt"l — acronym for *Zecher Tzaddik Livrochah* — blessed be the memory of a righteous one

Bibliography

Achad BeDoro, Rabbi Shmuel Kol, Tel Aviv, 5730

Acharon HaGeonim BeTunisia, C. Peretz, Bnei Brak, 5734

Admorei Belz, Yisrael Kalpholz, Yerushalayim, 5739

Al Mishkenos HaRoim, Machon Or Hatzfun, Yerushalayim

Anaf Eitz Avos, Rabbi Biyamin Menachem Alter

Aspaklaria HaMe'irah, Herschel Meshi-Zahav, Yerushalayim 5758

B'Tuv Yerushalayim, Rabbi Yitzchak Zev Goldberg, Yerushalayim, 5754

Baal Damesek Eliezer, Nosson Elya Roth, Bnei Brak, 5743

Baba Sali Rabbeinu HaKadosh, Rabbi Eliyahu Alfasi

Beis Karlin-Stolin, Yaakov Yisraeli (Kula), Tel Aviv

Beiso Na'avah Kodesh, Rabbi Efraim Pollack, Bnei Brak, 5753

Bikod Hachamah, Yerushalayim

Bishtei Einayim, Rabbi Moshe Sherer, New York, 5748

BiYeshishim Chochmah, Rabbi Noach Gad Weintraub, Yerushalayim, 5754

Butzina Kadisha, Alexander Sender Deutsch, Brooklyn, 5758

Chachmei Yisrael, Rabbi David Halachmi, Bnei Brak

Chevlei Yotzer, Aharon Soraski, Yerushalayim, 5734

Darkah shel Torah, Yerushalayim, 5759

Der Posek Hador, Menachem Mandel, Yerushalayim, 5754

Divrei Yeshuah V'Nechamah, Elazar Yehudah Leib Pinter

Gedolei Hadoros, Yechiel Michel Stern, Yerushalayim, 5756

Gur, Yitzchak Alfasi, Tel Aviv

HaBayis HaYehudi, Aharon Zakai, Yerushalayim, 5751

Hachuinuch B'darchei Avoseinu, Shimon Vanunu

HaEish Das, Shalom Meir HaKohen Wallach, 5754

HaGaon MiTchebin, Betzalel Landau, Yerushalayim, 5727

HaIsh Al HaChomah, Shlomo Zalman Sonenfeld, Yerushalayim 5735

Hakol La'Adon Hakol, R. Shain, Yerushalayim

Harav MiPonovich, Aharon Soraski, Bnei Brak, 5759

HaRebbi BeYisrael, Shikun Kretchnef, 5731

Hizaharu B'mamon Chaveireichem, Avraham Tovolski, Bnei Brak, 5741

HoAdmor MiSatmar, Avraham Fuchs, Yerushalayim, 5740

HoAdmor R' Avrohom Mordechai Alter MiGur, Rabbi Avraham Yitzchak Bromberg

Ish Chasidecha, Rabbi Betzalel Friedman, Yerushalayim, 5753

Ketzeis HaShemesh B'gvuraso, Avraham Tovolski, Bnei Brak, 5739

Kiryas Arba, Rabbi Elazar Klein, Be'er Sheva, 5722

*Kol Chotzev,*Machon Daas Torah, Yerushalayim, 5759

L'anavim Yitein Chein, Avraham Tovolski, Bnei Brak, 5739

Lapid HaEsh, Yechezkel Shraga Frankel, Bnei Brak 5750

Lev Eliyahu, Yerushalayim 5732

Libam shel Yisrael, Machon Amudei Haor, Yerushalayim, 5755

*Likkutei Yechezkel,*Bnei Brak, 5746

Maaseh Ish, Tzvi Yabrov, Bnei Brak, 5759

Marbitzei Torah Umussar, Aharon Soraski, Brooklyn, 5737

Maseches Avos – Yeina shel Torah, Rabbi Binyamin Adler, Yerushalayim, 5753

Meor Hachayim, Nosson Elya Roth, Bnei Brak 5750

Meor Yisrael, Aryeh Yehudah Harel, Yerushalayim, 5745

Meoran Shel Yisrael, Yehudah HaKohen Strasser and Aharon HaKohen Pearl, Brooklyn, 5752

Meori Galitzia – Encyclopedia L'chachmei Galicia, Rabbi Meir Wander, Yerushalayim, 5738

Meoros MeiOlam HaKabbalah VehaChasiddus, Yitzchak Alfasi, Tel Aviv

Midvar Sheker Tirchak, Avraham Tovolski, Bnei Brak, 5738

Migdolei Hachassidus, Rabbi Avraham Bromberg, Yerushalayim 5742

Mishel HaAvos, Rabbi Moshe Levi, Bnei Brak, 5752

Morei HaUmah, Rabbi Yisrael Shurin, New York

Moshian shel Yisrael, Shlomo Yaakov Gelbman, Kiryas Yoel, 5750

Ner Yisrael, Bnei Brak, 5759

Ohel Yosef, David Halachmi-Wiessbrod, Bnei Brak

Olam Chessed Yibaneh, Avraham Tovolski, Bnei Brak, 5748

Olamos Shecharvu, Rabbi Yosef Scheinberger, Yerushalayim, 5740

Orchos Chasidecha, Rabbi Asher Bergman, Bnei Brak, 5759

Oros Mimizrach, Aharon Soraski, Bnei Brak, 5734

Pe'er Hador, Rabbi Shlomo Cohen, Bnei Brak

Pe'er Ysirael, Baruch Vidislavski, Yerushalayim

Rabbeinu Zt"l MiGur, Biyamin Mintz, Yerushalayim, 5737

Rabboseinu, Rabbi Y. Avaraham Wolf, Bnei Brak, 5737

Reb Yaakov, Rabbi Nosson Kamenetzki

Ro'eh Even Yisrael, Avraham Zeev Schneebalg, Brooklyn, 5749

Rosh Golas Ariel, Avraham Mordechai Segal, Yerushalayim, 5755

Roshei Golas Ariel, Shlomo Rosman, 5736

Sama D'chayei, Avraham Tzvi Nashri, 5758

Sefer HoToldos, Rabbi Avrohom Chanoch Glitzenstein, Kfar Chabad, 5736

She'al Avicha VeYagedcha, Yisrael Spiegel, Yerushalayim, 5757

Shefer Harereiu Kedem, Shlomo Rosman, 5751

Shem Hagdolim L'gedolei Hungaria, Yerushalayim Publications, Brooklyn, 5718

Shmuel B'doro, Machon Shem Mishmuel, Brooklyn

Sichos Chaim, Rabbi Nosson Chaim Einfeld, Bnei Brak, 5759

Tiferes Yoel, Elimelech Ozer Bodek, Brooklyn, 5753

Toldos Aharon, Mordechai HaKohen Blum, Yerushalayim, 5752

Torah Yevakshu MiPihu, 5760

Uvda D'Aharon, Eliyahu Kohen Steinberger, Yerushalayim, 5754

Uvdos V'hanhagos L'Beis Brisk, Shimon Yosef Meller, Yerushalayim 5759

VaYechi Yosef, Aharon Soraski, Yerushalayim, 5756

VeZos Lihudah, Aharon Soraski, Yerushalayim, 5756

Yeshivos Hungaria B'gdulasan Uvchurbanan, Avraham Fuchs,
   Yerushalayim, 5739

Zaharei Chamah, Mashabim, Yerushalayim, 5742

Zichron Tzaddik, Yitzchak Isaac Zelikovitz, Yerushalayim, 5747

Zikaron BaSefer, Yonah Landau, Brooklyn, 5741

Index of Personalities

לזכר עולם יהיה צדיק

לעילוי נשמת מורי ורבי
רבן של ישראל
גאון ישראל וקדושו
מרן רבי אהרן קוטלר זצוקללה"ה

הוא הגבר הקים עולה של תורה, עת אמריקה היתה עוד מדבר שממה, עבד בלי ליאות בעד חינוך התורני בארצינו הקדושה, בהקמת מוסדות התורה בכל עיירה קטנה וגדולה.

אהבתו לתורה לא ידעה גבולות, מעודו לא שח שיחה בטילה אפילו לרגעים ספורות, בימי זעם ועברה התמסר כולו להצלת נפשות יקרות, לחם בעד כל קוץ ותג של מסורת אבות, להגיד שבחו של אהרן שלא שינה משנים קדמוניות.

ראש ישיבת קלעצק המעטירה, ואחר חורבן אירופה, יסד את לייקוואוד עיר התורה, ובו בזמן שימש כראש ישיבת עץ חיים בירושלים קריה נאמנה, כולם שוים לטובה.

חידושי תורתו נתחדשו בעמלות עצומה, בעיון בהלכה באגדה ובספרי יראה, ומסרם לתלמידיו באהבה גלויה, "כל חפציך לא ישוו בה" כפשוטה, ללמוד וללמד לשמור ולעשות ולקיים בקדושה ובטהרה.

אש תמיד יקדה בקרבו אהבה בתענוגים, הרביץ תורה יותר מיובל שנים, העמיד תלמידים לאלפי אלפים, הממשיכים במסירת התורה לעדרי עדרים, כנבואת אבי חוזה שלא תשכח התורה לעולמים.

עלה בסערה השמימה ב' כסליו, תשכ"ג

יהי רצון שימליץ טוב בעדינו להיושע בישועת עולמים

ת. נ. צ. ב. ה.

לזכר שלם יהיה צדיק

לעילוי נשמת מורי ורבי
רבן של ישראל גאון ישראל וקדושו
מרן רבי אליעזר זוסיא פארטוגאל זצוקללה"ה
כ"ק אדמור מסקולען

משחר ימיו עבד את בוראו במסירות נפלאה, לאהב
את השם בכל מקום עולם ומלואה, בתענוגי בשרים מאס רק במצות ה' התנאה,
ובמיוחד בקבלת עול מלכותו בדביקות נפלאה.

אהבתו לעם סגולתו לא ידעה גבולות, כל מקום בואו השיב לב בנים על אבות,
בסקולען בטשערנאוויץ ובבוקארעסט הקים מוסדות למופת,"ואת הנפש אשר עשו
בחרן" בה הראה נפלאות.

דיין אלמנות ואבי יתומים, שנשארו לפליטה בודדים וגלמודים, בביתו גידלם מתוך
אהבה בלי מצרים, ביחד עם הרבנית הצדקנית, מחברתו בחיים, כאב וכאם התמסרו
בלי גבולים ומעצורים.

האב ובנו נתיסרו בגיהנם עלי אדמות, ועונו בעינויים מרים כלענות, וגם שם בגיא
צלמות, לבו ובשרו רננו שירים ותשבחות לנורא עלילות.

בצאתו מארץ הדמים, תיכף שם לילות כימים, להצלת אחיו הנדכאים, אסירי עני
וברזל תחת עול הקומוניסטים, ובעבור צור עולמים, הציל המון אנשים והביאם לחוף
מבטחים.

בראותו כל עיר על תלה בנויה ועיר אלהים מושפלת עד שאול תחתיה, תיכף יסד
מוסדות חסד לאברהם לשם ולתהלה, תורה ותעודה וכלי החמדה, ילדי חמד הוגי
תורה, עטרה ליושנה להחזיר כבתחילה.

עלה בסערה השמימה ער"ח אלול, תשמ"ב
יהי רצון שימליץ טוב בעדינו להיושע בישועת עולמים

ת. נ. צ. ב. ה.